Church Shopping

IN THE BAY AREA

Church Shopping

IN THE BAY AREA

*A Guide to Finding a Spiritual Home
for Nonbelievers, Seekers, and Others*

BARBARA STEVENSON

SASQUATCH BOOKS
SEATTLE

Printed in the United States of America.
Distributed in Canada by Raincoast Books Ltd.
07 06 05 04 02 02 01   5 4 3 2 1

Cover and interior design: Kate Basart
Cover illustration: Jack A. Molloy
Composition: Jenny Semet
Copy editor: Rebecca Pepper
Proofreader: Sigrid Asmus

Library of Congress Cataloging in Publication Data
Stevenson, Barbara, 1954–
Church shopping in the Bay Area : a guide to finding a spiritual home for nonbelievers,
seekers, and others / Barbara Stevenson—San Francisco Bay Area ed.
p. cm.
Includes index.
ISBN 1-57061-233-1
1. Protestant churches—California—San Francisco Bay Area. San Francisco Bay Area
(Calif.)—Religious life and customs. 3. Non church-affiliated people—Religious life—
California—San Francisco Bay Area. I. Title.

BR560.S3 S74 2001
277.94'61083—dc21

Sasquatch Books
615 Second Avenue
Seattle, Washington 98104
(206) 467-4300
books@SasquatchBooks.com
www.SasquatchBooks.com

DEDICATION

To Mom and Dad, with love and thanks

Contents

PART TWO

PART THREE

Acknowledgments

I owe profound thanks to Jennie McDonald, whose clever idea this book was in the first place. She also had a big role in the design of the project and was instrumental in its execution.

I am also deeply grateful to the many clergy people who took the time to help me gather data about individual churches by filling out a questionnaire. Not only did a number of pastors go to great lengths to return information in time for my deadline, they were also generous with their words of support and encouragement.

To the community of St. Aidan's Episcopal Church, San Francisco: many, many thanks for showing me the way.

Introduction

When I was ten years old, my brother Patrick, who was then five, fell head-first from the upstairs porch of our house onto the concrete driveway two stories below. I saw him fall. It was a sunny summer morning, and I had been making my bed. Facing the door of my room, I had a clear view into my brothers' room across the hall. The door from the boys' room to the porch was open and I paused for a moment to look at something outside—a bird I heard singing or maybe just the sunlight on the leaves of the maple tree out front. So I happened to see Patrick leaning over the railing, and I watched his feet rise up from the floor and then disappear. I don't remember hearing him land, but I do remember standing for a moment, frozen in horror, before I ran downstairs screaming for my mother. The next thing I knew, my mother had disappeared, off to the emergency room, leaving my older sister Susan in charge of the five of us who remained.

Convinced that Patrick was seriously injured or even dying, we huddled together, feeling scared and miserable. Eileen and Katy started crying. Someone suggested that we pray for Patrick, and someone else thought maybe we should even go to church. So Susan bundled the baby into a stroller, and off we trooped.

Mom brought Patrick home a few hours later. We all thought it bordered on the miraculous that Patrick had escaped with only a sprained ankle, but we didn't quite dare to believe that our prayers had had any effect on the outcome. The incident found its way into the family mythology as "the time Patrick fell off the upstairs porch and we all went to church (on a day not a Sunday! all by ourselves!) to pray." As the years passed, the retelling of the tale carried an increasingly rueful tone, as if we had been caught overreacting.

Despite its anticlimactic ending, this was one of the most profound experiences of my childhood. Thirty-five years later, I remember how unbearably powerless I felt in the face of what I was certain would be a great tragedy. I also recall the intensity of the relief I felt going into the dim and empty church, lighting a candle in front of the familiar plaster statue of the Virgin Mary, and kneeling down to pray.

I never was convinced that praying did any good; I just knew it made me feel better. Sometime during my high school years, I came to believe that mentally vocalizing the words "Please God, please God, please . . ." in moments of distress was pathetic. So my prayer life, such as it was, ceased to be. Church for me was of a piece with the conservative and sometimes harsh Irish Catholic culture in which I was raised. When I left my parents' house to live on my own, I gleefully threw it all off. I don't think I went to church on any occasion other than Christmas—or for any reason other than to sing Christmas carols—for nearly twenty years.

Over those years, I toyed occasionally with the question of whether or not I believed in God, but I never felt compelled to come up with a firm answer. I didn't have much of a spiritual life. Yet I always carried with me the memory of my frightened ten-year-old self. I knew that when I had a child of my own I would want her to have something to turn to when she found herself feeling as afraid and helpless as I had.

When my daughter was two years old, I finally got around to looking for a faith community. I started by drawing up a list of requirements: Walking distance from my house in San Francisco would be a big plus. I knew I wanted a progressive community. I also had this vaguely formed idea that I was looking for a cerebral church, one that offered intelligent sermons from the pulpit and restrained behavior from the pews—a vision that I've since recognized as something remarkably like worship cum National Public Radio. I didn't really expect to find a church for me, a spiritually retarded, cranky, lefty intelligentsia fellow traveler. I set out on this search thinking that the best I could hope for was a church that Rosie would like and I could tolerate.

My husband and I began to look in fits and starts. We went to Christmas Eve services at one church, Christmas morning services at another, Easter at yet another. Then we didn't get out of bed on Sunday morning for months a time. When we began to go out and visit churches regularly, we soon developed the ability to quickly recognize what we liked and what we didn't. I also came to realize that what we were doing was not unusual in the Bay Area—it even had a name, "church shopping." (I actually find this term a somewhat incongruous choice for a process that so many people turn to as an antidote to consumerism, but its efficiency is irresistible, so I use it.)

Our search was not as logical and orderly as I thought it would be, and its results were completely unexpected. Like so many other big life choices—deciding where to live, finding a preschool—we began with an orderly plan, modified it as we gathered more information from direct observation, and waited to feel the click that comes with recognizing something that's right for us. David and I thought we were looking for an old church with formal architecture, an impressive choir, lots of gorgeous organ music, and a huge Sunday school program. I was anticipating (since the whole reason for doing this was my child, not me) that I would drop Rosie off in Sunday school and then go into the sanctuary and zone out—listen to music, have quiet time to myself, be virtually invisible and definitely untouchable. I was also looking forward to actually going to church maybe two Sundays out of four, taking advantage of what I'd always thought of as the niftiest feature of Protestantism, optional attendance.

The parish that has been our church home for nearly ten years is a small congregation in a building that was built in the 1960s. There isn't a stained glass window in the place. The choir is so far from professional that they let me join, and we have piano or guitar accompaniment more often than organ music. Church school is a one-room-schoolhouse program, with an average Sunday attendance of six kids between the ages of four and ten. The only requirement on my original list that this church meets is its distance from home: It's only a mile—of course, every single step of that distance is straight uphill.

When we first went to Sunday morning services at St. Aidan's, I fought back tears every week during the Prayers of the People, when members of the congregation speak out loud the concerns and fears in their hearts. And in this parish people hug each other, rather than shake hands, in the part of the service where you "exchange the peace." It happened very quickly, and I'm still not entirely sure how, but for the past ten years I have been going to church every Sunday morning (and occasionally on weekday evenings as well). I have taught Sunday school, chaired the liturgy committee, edited the newsletter, and even served on the board.

The astonishing thing about all of this is that I haven't really changed. I didn't have a conversion experience, and I still don't pray. I'm the same skeptical, sarcastic, befuddled ex-anarchist I was ten years ago. I recently realized that I focused on Sunday school for my daughter when I went looking for a church because I didn't think I was church material. I see now that my plan to remain remote and uninvolved stemmed from my conviction that I would be assuming a false persona when I went to church. After all, if the church folk got to know who I really was, they'd surely kick me out. And that doesn't even begin to touch on how unlikely it seemed that I would ever find true soul mates among, well, church-goers.

But I found a church that embraces me and enriches my life in countless ways. My son was baptized into a community of people who had watched him grow inside me, in a ceremony that was one of the most deeply moving events of my adult life. Both my children discuss God with a matter-of-fact ease that I find enviable. Our family holiday traditions, anchored in the rituals of the church, now have a weight that I love. And virtually all of my friends who are a lot younger or a lot older than I, who have different-colored skin, or who have a lot less or a lot more money than I do are people I know from church.

Many of us fear that our true selves—with our sexual preferences, our gender politics, or our aesthetic and intellectual standards—will be awkward and unwelcome guests behind church doors on Sunday morning. This simply isn't true. Whoever you are, and whatever your reason for seeking out a faith community, somewhere in the Bay Area there is a church for you.

Maybe you're like me and you grew up in a church-going family, but the faith of your youth doesn't work for you anymore, even though you want the benefits of religious instruction and rituals for your kids. Maybe you have never gone to church regularly but find yourself yearning for spiritual support as you face midlife. Maybe you want to find an avenue for doing some good in the world. Maybe you're simply looking for community. Whatever your reason, you can find a church that enriches your life as profoundly as St. Aidan's has enriched mine.

I haven't tried to be comprehensive in this book. There are no data here on Jewish temples, Catholic churches, fundamentalist congregations, or churches that minister to culturally specific communities in their native language. Perhaps it's the influence of my thirteen years with the nuns, but I think that for most of us it's only the mainline Protestant denominations that are vaguely interchangeable. If you are looking for a synagogue or a Buddhist temple, you don't need this book; the Yellow Pages will locate the handful of choices in your community, and visiting them all is a feasible task. Along those same lines, if you're a practicing Catholic or born-again Christian, your search for a church home will not take you down the path I've outlined here.

This book is written for people who feel, as I did, so disconnected from organized religion that they don't know where to start. (My father calls these people "heathens," but I believe the seminary term is "unchurched.") When we heathens set out to find a faith community, the particular denomination of the congregation we settle in is not the prime factor in our choice. What's important to us—whether it's acceptance of same-sex relationships and alternative families, language that doesn't offend our feminist beliefs, dedication to peace and social justice, support for spiritual seeking, or a host of other idiosyncratic preferences—can be found in individual communities sprinkled throughout the mainline denominations. My search happened to begin and end in the denomination in which my husband grew up. But I am certain that, had we not found the particular Episcopal parish we settled on, we would have found a Presbyterian or a Lutheran or a Methodist or a United Church of Christ or American Baptist congregation that suited us just as well, and would have suited us much better than numerous other Episcopal congregations would have.

The process of church shopping is different for us heathens, and this book is designed to make your search a rewarding and successful one. Part One of the book describes the process of church shopping in general terms: how to select churches to visit, what to look for when you do visit, what to expect when you attend a church service for the first time, social elements you are likely to encounter, and how to join a church once you've found one you like. Part Two covers the particulars of finding a church for each of three groups of people: families with children; lesbians, gays, bisexuals, and transgendered individuals (LGBT for short); and political progressives and/or cultural creatives. You may, of course, fall into more than one of these categories, in which case you will want to read all of the relevant sections. Part Three includes data on approximately four hundred congregations, including contact information and the hours of Sunday worship services. In addition, there are twenty-two lists that sort the congregations by attributes. You can use these lists as clues to find a church that meets your particular needs. This part of the book also contains a glossary of terms that you may encounter in your search.

When I set out to go church shopping, I was apprehensive and rather confused. If I'd known then what I know now, it wouldn't have taken me so long to start looking, and it would have taken me a lot less time to find my church home. It is my hope that this guide will reduce your confusion, eliminate your apprehension, and lead you to the good news (see the Glossary, page 195) that's waiting for you.

PART ONE

General advice on searching for a church: Descriptions of practices common to different denominations, practical tips on how to behave gracefully during a service, emotional support to overcome your doubts and fears

Getting Started

Of course, I quite agree that the Christian religion is, in the long run, a thing of unspeakable comfort. But it does not begin in comfort; it begins in dismay.

—FROM *Mere Christianity* BY C.S. LEWIS

Even if you put aside the spiritual needs that are driving you to seek out a faith community, getting going on your church-shopping adventure can be a dismaying prospect. If you wanted to feel sorry for yourself, you could lament the fact that the relatively low percentage of church-goers among Bay Area residents (and yes, I think this quality is part of our unique and so charming character) makes it unlikely you will have the luxury of a friend's company when you venture on church visits.

Mustering your courage to show up at a place you've never been before to interact with a group of people you've never before met—who, worse yet, all know each other very well—is hard enough. The really scary thoughts, though, the ones that can keep you home on Sunday mornings for a very long time, are all the fears you have about entering this foreign culture. It is probably not an accident that you haven't darkened the door of a church in many years, if at all. Although you may believe that church is where you will find some things you want and need very much, it is easy to get lost in trepidation. What will I do if everyone starts talking about Jeeeeeeezus? Are they going to ask me what I believe? I'm afraid I'm going to feel like a freak!

What you have to do is breathe deeply and take the plunge. I wish I could assure you that you will not feel a moment's unease. The fact of the matter is that church is in many ways its own subculture, with its own peculiar vocabulary and habits, and the more sensitive among us can find exposure to them an off-putting experience. In the most progressive, artsy, open-minded congregations around you will hear some words that might make you cringe. Every time I hear "fellowship," for example, I squirm a little, in an involuntary and not especially defensible reaction somehow tied to a not very nice afternoon I spent with a bunch of overly aggressive Hare Krishnas twenty-five years ago. The trick is to realize that every subculture has buzzwords and the smartest thing to do is to accept them in their own context. Just think of all the new vocabulary words we've learned from Internet companies. When a group of people who are trying to do great things together have worked out something important, usually as a result of much discussion and experimentation, they come up with a new name for it. They use the new term, rather than an everyday word, because the new name acts as efficient shorthand for a set of specific understandings and nuances. Thus, for example, churches don't use the word "community," which many of us ex-hippie types are perfectly comfortable with, because it doesn't include important conceptual elements that "the body of Christ" does. And "community building" is too vague for churches, who distinguish between "evangelism" (focused on people who aren't a part of the church) and "stewardship" (oriented toward members of the church). If you are one who has trouble with this specialized language, have patience. Didn't you find "bandwidth" irritating when it first started popping up? Do you blink an eye when you hear it now?

There's also no getting around the fact that you are going to hear the name Jesus quite a bit. For a liberal intellectual worker like myself, starting to go to church was an exercise in shedding negative cultural assumptions about Christianity. I was doing pretty well, too. I took note of how many intelligent people with good taste I met at church, I observed some utterly uncompromising critical thinkers living their spiritual quests within the community of the church, I took particular note of the genuine acceptance I myself experienced. But whenever the name Jesus came up, I would get very, very nervous.

Jesus is what Christianity is all about, after all. What I didn't know before, however, is that plenty of people who fervently believe in the resurrected Christ are unconcerned about whether or not the historical figure actually existed. They read the Bible as wisdom literature and consider Christianity to be one of many possible pathways to the truth. To them, "Jesus" represents a way of being in the world that is all about joy and delight and has nothing to do with condemning others. The Eucharist is not the literal transubstantiation of bread and wine into the body and blood of Christ; it is a ritual for reminding one another of the oneness of humanity.

So be prepared and be open—don't panic and bolt when you visit a church that talks about Jesus a lot, because they all do. Don't be afraid of a church that describes itself as "Christ-centered," and don't write off churches just because they celebrate Communion every Sunday. There are plenty of people who are smarter than you are who pray to Jesus and take irony-free Communion every week.

After you have gotten over your own discomfort, you will still need to deal with the dismayed reactions of your friends. In a progressive-minded region like the Bay Area where most people have no immediate personal experience of church-going, the images of Christian churches that are in general circulation flow from the Christian Right. Even acquaintances of church-going folks who are just as forward-thinking as the next person find it all too easy to think "self-righteous" and "conservative" and "homophobic" when the word "church" comes up. If you are lucky enough to have friends who are aware that all church-goers are not abortion clinic bombers, you might find that they do believe that everybody who goes to church is either hopelessly sentimental or not very bright. Many of my friends do.

Integrating being Christian into my own definition of myself was challenging, but going public with the church thing was excruciating. For most of my adult life I kept the whole idea of church in the mental file cabinet I have set aside for family affairs—that place in my mind where I keep visits to my parents, my New Jersey cousins' tacky weddings in Knights of Columbus Halls, and the secrets I share with my siblings. When I chose to get married by a priest and to have my first child baptized, despite the fact that I wasn't going to church more than twice a year, I tucked those two events away, neatly separated from my normal reality, and shut the drawer.

When we started attending every Sunday, however, church began to migrate from the dusty corner of my emotional attic to the main floor of my everyday life, and consequently to come up in conversation once in a while. I'd mention the c-word, for instance, when I turned down an invitation for a Sunday-morning social event. In a conversation about some random bit of information I'd acquired I would confess that it came from the rector's sermon the previous week.

A certain number of people, both old friends and new acquaintances, looked at me with a mixture of confusion and just a touch of horror. More often I met with a thoughtful reassessment, more along the lines of "Well, that's something I would never have suspected about you" than "Yikes! Get me out of here." Some folks wanted to drop the subject as quickly as possible, but I was amazed by how many people were interested in hearing more about the whys and hows of my church-going, even among my acquaintances who are most hostile to organized religion. What I had forgotten is that anyone who is on a spiritual quest—and, when it comes down to it, that description could apply to virtually every thoughtful person I know—is naturally interested in the journeys of others. Open-minded people recognize that we are looking for the same answers, although we might be framing the questions differently. Prepared to be surprised.

You can begin the first phase of your search, the armchair phase, even while you are still mired in doubts and fears and not yet committed to the idea of finding a faith community. What follows is a series of recommendations for how to think about what kind of church you might want to look for if—and a suggested process for when—you decide to jump into this adventure. There is no science to this endeavor, so feel free to ignore any or all of these suggestions. If this approach seems overly prescriptive, you might want to read the rest of this chapter through for a general idea of the questions you might consider and then invent your own method. The objective of this preliminary investigation is to come up with a list of churches that you can start sampling.

DECIDE WHAT'S MOST IMPORTANT TO YOU

Once you've either selected or eliminated denominations from your list of possibilities, you should decide what you're going to use as your primary "search tool" for a church. What's most important to you? Honor whatever it is that comes forward when you ask yourself this question, no matter how inconsequential it might seem. If you yearn to hear a big organ, don't talk yourself into being practical and going to the little church down the street, which most often has guitar music. On the other hand, if the last thing you want to do on Sunday morning is travel across town, don't feel shy about putting geography at the top of your list. When you have decided what's most important, use that one element as your selection tool to draw up the preliminary list of churches that might be a good match for you.

CONSIDER DENOMINATION

Even though there is a great deal of diversity among individual congregations in a given national church, thinking about denomination is helpful. Do you have any preferences, either for or against, any of the mainline branches? Some people find that they want to flee as far as possible from the church they've known in the past, while others want exactly the same experience they had growing up or something just a little bit different. The Episcopal church works for me because so many of the liturgical elements are similar to the Catholic rituals I remember from my childhood, yet the church is different in several ways—in having women priests, for example—that are important to me.

On paper, the mainline "flavors" of Protestantism (Lutheran, Presbyterian, Episcopal, Methodist, Baptist, Congregationalist or UCC) seem very similar. All Protestants share three fundamental beliefs, which stem from their common roots in the sixteenth-century protest against the Catholic Church of the time: (1) a belief that you are individually responsible to God, whose grace comes to you through Christ as a gift, which cannot be bought or earned; (2) a belief in the authority of the Bible; and (3) a belief in the universal priesthood of all believers, which means that you don't need a mediator, such as a priest, between you and God. They all celebrate the core sacraments of baptism and Communion (also known as the Lord's Supper and the Eucharist).

There are also definite differences, however, and you might find that you are drawn to one denomination over another. Some people with no sustained exposure to organized religion are intellectually intrigued by the historical roots of a particular denomination—for instance, you might like the idea of joining the church that is a direct descendant of Martin Luther, who started it all—and begin by looking there. Or maybe you once knew a minister who impressed you, so you begin your search in her denomination. If you think you want to send your children to a parochial school someday, you might begin with the Lutherans, who are well known for their educational institutions. If, like my brother Tom, formal ritual of any kind makes you feel like a ten-year-old under the ruthless eye of a stern father, you will want to avoid Episcopalians, who do love their vestments and processions.

Part Three of this book includes an overview of the Big Five mainline national churches (Episcopal, Lutheran, Presbyterian, Methodist, Baptist) and two smaller denominations that come out of the very interesting Congregationalist tradition, the United Church of Christ and the Disciples of Christ. Reading about them all might help you determine whether or not you have a preference for one denomination over another. Most of the national church bodies have excellent web sites (the URLs are included in the Part Three overview), with sections designed for church shoppers that answer questions about the tradition's beliefs and practices. Many of them also have "church locators," which allow you to find individual congregations by state, area, or even zip code.

USE THIS BOOK TO GET STARTED
Part One of this book has information that will be of use to everyone: a peek behind the front door to see what a Sunday morning service looks like, a preview of the kind of reception you're likely to get as a visitor, and some helpful hints on how to figure out what's going on.

Part Two has more in-depth information for three groups of people—

families with young children; gays, lesbians, bisexuals, transgendered individuals, singles, and alternative families; and political progressives and cultural creatives. Each of these groups has a chapter full of specific advice and information, including a description of the attributes of churches that most often correlate to a high degree of satisfaction for people in that group.

Part Three has basic contact information for most of the congregations of the five mainline denominations, as well as the United Church of Christ and the Disciples of Christ, within San Francisco, San Mateo, Santa Clara, Marin, and Alameda Counties. I also distributed a questionnaire to these churches that asked each congregation for information about its staff, programs, and practices. I have used the data collected from the questionnaires to create a series of lists, grouping together congregations that share certain key qualities.

COME UP WITH A SHORT LIST

When you've decided which interest group you most identify with (and if it's one of the three I discuss in depth), read that chapter in Part Two and decide which attributes you're looking for in a church. If none of the three identities fits, read all three chapters to come up with your own customized list of the attributes you'll be seeking. Look in Part Three for churches with those attributes and start making a list of likely congregations. Then shorten your list a bit by layering in another round of preferences.

Do you have a decided partiality for big or small settings? Large churches, like large schools and large companies, often have resources that are out of the reach of small congregations—professional choirs, comprehensive education programs, groups for every imaginable interest and age group. Some of us, though, love the intimacy and immediacy of small-scale institutions and will choose them every time. Others of us have a mixture of experiences in our lives: Maybe you work for a Fortune 500 corporation but also volunteer many hours as the board president of a grassroots community group. Consider whether you have a preference for a big or small church.

How about dress code? I have a friend who loves getting decked out for church. Having grown up in a church-going family of six girls, she feels an emotional link to her childhood when she puts on her heels and makeup every Sunday morning. When she was church shopping, she was wise enough to honor that preference and visited churches whose members like to dress up. My husband and I, on the other hand, both remember the ritual of scrambling into our Sunday best as weekly torture sessions. We take delight in the astonished looks we get from friends who goggle at our jeans and sneakers and ask, "You went to church dressed like that!?" Of course, churches don't have formal dress codes and you will see a range of styles in most congregations. But you will also note a predominant tone, and it's something to pay attention to if you have strong feelings about what you wear to church.

Then there's music. For some people, music is way down on the list of priorities, while for others it is one of the most important parts of a church service. There are some obvious things to think about here: organ music versus more eclectic instrumentation, the size and quality of the choir, classical versus contemporary, the priority a given congregation assigns to music. But there are also some less obvious, even counterintuitive, questions you should ask yourself about what you want. Do you mainly like to listen, or do you really want to sing? Many churches with large choirs and outstanding music programs have a higher percentage of "performance" pieces sung by the choir without participation from the rest of the congregation. Listening to beautiful music, beautifully sung, is exactly what many people want. But for others of us—even my friend Eileen, who as far as I can tell is completely tone deaf—being able to participate is more important than the quality of the sound that ensues. For those people, a church with a more home-grown music program, in which the congregation as a whole makes all the music, is a better fit.

After considering this additional layer of preference, make up a short list of churches that, at least on paper, look like your best prospects. (Hang on to that long list, though. You may need to return to it.)

AN OVERVIEW OF MAINLINE PROTESTANT DENOMINATIONS

Many American national churches are the products of mergers, sometimes a series of mergers over hundreds of years. The list of antecedents under each denomination gives the previously independent denominations that fed into each modern-day national church. Historical figures are the founders or theological forbears associated with the denomination. Some religions, like Lutheran and Baptist, have more than one national body within their tradition. In this book I have chosen to focus on the more progressive wings, but the other branches are listed so that you know what they are.

Lutheran

PRIMARY NATIONAL BODY: Evangelical Lutheran Church of America, or ELCA (5.2 million members, 10,851 congregations).

ANTECEDENTS: American Lutheran Church, Lutheran Church of America, Association of Evangelical Lutheran Churches.

HISTORY AND HISTORICAL FIGURES: Martin Luther, after whom Lutheranism is named, was the German monk widely recognized as the "father of Protestantism." While studying for the priesthood, he got really ticked off by the difference between what he was reading in the Bible and the actual church practices he saw in the world around him. On October 31, 1517, he posted his 95 Theses on the church doors at Wittenberg University, challenging the church to a debate on the issues he had identified. Some of the changes he wanted to make (other than the obvious ones, like rooting out graft and corruption) were to conduct worship services in the language of the people and to get rid of indulgences, the practice by which people could reduce the time they were destined to serve in purgatory by paying money to the church, reciting certain prayers, and doing certain acts.

Over the centuries, Lutheranism took an especially strong hold in Germany and Scandinavia, and Lutherans in America for many years cohered in groups that reflected their nationalities and relied very heavily on the Old Country for clergy and worship materials. In the twentieth century the ethnic churches began to merge into successively bigger national church bodies, until the latest merger in 1988 created the Evangelical Lutheran Church in America, the fourth largest Protestant church in the country. The ELCA is in "full communion," which means they are ready to do lots of things together, even swap clergy, with the

Lutheran World Federation, the Episcopal Church USA, the Presbyterian Church USA, the Moravian Church in America, the Reformed Church in America, and the United Church of Christ.

FAMOUS FOR: Lutheran churches in general are well known for their Christian education. Many of them have very strong Sunday school programs, and a number have parish schools, mostly preschool and elementary, as well.

OTHER NATIONAL LUTHERAN CHURCHES: I am always tempted to think, when I see the word "evangelical," that it indicates a more conservative or fundamentalist orientation. That isn't the case here: "Evangelical" refers to a historic American religious tradition that folded into the ELCA. In fact the Lutheran Church–Missouri Synod (LCMS), the other national Lutheran church, is the more conservative. LCMS holds to a more literal belief in the Bible and the historic sixteenth-century Lutheran confessional writings; it also believes that to be in fellowship with other Christians—to do things like share worship services and Communion—you need to agree with them on everything the Bible teaches. Communion at an LCMS worship service, therefore, is offered to LCMS members only. Because of its more conservative nature, I haven't included LCMS congregations in the lists of churches at the back of this book.

WEB SITE: The ELCA web site at www.elca.org has interesting background literature on Lutheranism and the history of the ELCA. It also has a church locator, which allows you to type in your zip code, specify a distance, and have it search out the ELCA congregations within that radius of your home. You can call up locations by state or city as well. Once you've found a list of local churches you're interested in, you can get a brief summary of statistics about them, such as total membership, average Sunday attendance, and the number of Sunday school students.

Presbyterian

PRIMARY NATIONAL BODY: The Presbyterian Church USA, or PCUSA (2.5 million members in 11,216 congregations).

ANTECEDENTS: Presbyterian Church in the United States, United Presbyterian Church in the USA.

HISTORY AND HISTORICAL FIGURES: John Calvin was the French/Swiss theologian who came along about twenty years after Luther's 95 Theses and refined the reform way of thinking about God and God's relationship to humanity into what became known as "reformed theology." John Knox, a Scot who studied with Calvin in Switzerland, took Calvin's teachings back to Scotland, where they were widely adopted and spread into England.

"Presbyterian" comes from the Greek word for "elder." The pattern of church government that Calvin developed, which remains a distinguishing characteristic of the church today, vests governing authority in elected lay persons known as elders.

The Presbyterian Church in the United States split apart and reunited several times over the years. PCUSA was formed in 1983 when the United Presbyterian Church in the USA (PCUS), or the "southern branch," merged with the "northern branch," the United Presbyterian Church in the USA (UPCUSA). Other, smaller national bodies still extant include the Presbyterian Church in America, the Cumberland Presbyterian Church, and the Associate Reformed Presbyterian Churches.

FAMOUS FOR: Presbyterians are justifiably proud of their tradition of lay leadership and democracy. There is no such thing as a pastor deciding what's going down and telling the congregation what to do. Individual congregations are governed by a body of lay leaders known as the session of elders. Presbyterian theology also emphasizes service, so Presbyterian churches are known for having many active outreach programs.

WEB SITE: The PCUSA web site at www.pcusa.org not only has a church locator into which you enter your zip code or SCF (the first three digits of your zip code) and get a list of nearby churches, it also provides ten years' worth of data on membership, average Sunday attendance, and church school enrollment for all of the individual churches, available as either a bar graph or a table.

Methodist

PRIMARY NATIONAL BODY: United Methodist Church (8.6 million members, 36,771 congregations).

ANTECEDENTS: Church of the United Brethren in Christ, Evangelical Association, Evangelical United Brethren Church, Methodist Church.

HISTORY AND HISTORICAL FIGURES: John Wesley and his brother Charles spent so much time in methodical prayer and Bible reading at Oxford that they were mocked as "Methodists," no doubt by the eighteenth-century equivalent of party-hearty frat boys. Both brothers went to Georgia as Church of England missionaries in 1736 but returned home after a short time, seriously discouraged. In 1738 they led a lively renewal movement in the Church of England and eventually started sending lay preachers as missionaries to the British colonies. After the Revolutionary War, John Wesley began ordaining ministers to send to the colonies, paving the way for the establishment of Methodism as its own denomination.

Meanwhile, two other churches were being founded in primarily German-speaking American communities. Philip William Otterbein and Martin Boehm began the Church of United Brethren in Christ, and some years later Jacob Albright, a Lutheran who was attracted to the Methodist tradition, founded the Evangelical Association. Through a succession of mergers, the most recent in 1968, these three American traditions came together in the United Methodist Church.

FAMOUS FOR: Personal discipline and social responsibility are core values for the Methodist tradition. Thus, some of the best-known church social service programs in a given area—Glide Memorial, for instance—are Methodist. The church also maintains its historic temperance positions on alcohol, drugs, and tobacco, supporting (rather than mandating) abstinence as "a faithful witness to God's liberating and redeeming love for persons."

WEB SITE: The web site at www.umc.org has a church locator that will provide you with the names and contact information for churches in your city or zip code. It also provides some additional data for each church, but the information is sketchy compared to the Presbyterian and Lutheran web sites. It contains a very thorough history of the church and statements of church policy on a number of theological and social issues.

Episcopalian

PRIMARY NATIONAL BODY: The Episcopal Church USA, or ECUSA (2.5 million members, 7,500 congregations).

ANTECEDENTS: Church of England.

HISTORY AND HISTORICAL FIGURES: Episcopalians are members of the Anglican Communion, the association of national churches around the world that grew out of the original Church of England, whose spiritual head is the Archbishop of Canterbury. The Episcopal Church is named after the Greek word for "bishop," which just goes to show how much importance Episcopalians place on the "historic episcopate"—they believe they can trace their bishops' spiritual heritage in an unbroken line to the first apostles of Jesus. As Episcopalian literature so diplomatically phrases it, the Church of England was founded in the sixteenth century, when the church "moved away from being ruled by the Pope" yet did not reject its Catholic roots as a number of other Protestant traditions did. The disagreement arose when Pope Clement

VII refused to allow Henry VIII to end his marriage to Catherine of Aragon and marry Anne Boleyn. English kings of the time, accustomed as they were to having a state religion, expected to be able to call a certain number of shots on the church front. Through a series of legal maneuvers and arm-twisting, Henry ultimately had Parliament declare the king, rather than the Pope, to be the head of the church in England. When the American colonies officially became a new country in 1789, the Church of England founded its first church on our shores.

FAMOUS FOR: Reflecting the Anglican identity as being a "via media" or middle way between Protestantism and the Catholic Church, Episcopalian worship is reminiscent in many respects of Catholic masses. The priests wear vestments, the Eucharist is a central part of virtually every service, and some congregations even go for "smells and bells," or incense and bell ringing.

WEB SITE: www.ecusa.org has a very nice question-and-answer section that tells you about the Episcopal Church. There's no church locator, unfortunately, although you can look for the web sites of churches near you, and most congregations do have a web site. It also has links to a variety of Anglican web sites, including the very lively Anglicans Online.

Baptist

PRIMARY NATIONAL BODY: Baptists as a whole are the largest Protestant denomination in the United States, with 26 million members. About half of them belong to the Baptist Southern Convention (BSC). Even though the BSC is the biggest group, it's also among the most conservative, so I've chosen to focus in this book on the more liberal national group, the American Baptist Churches USA (1.5 million members, 5,800 congregations).

HISTORY AND ANTECEDENTS: The earliest Baptist leader was John Smyth, a Church of England minister who went to the Netherlands in 1607 and founded a Baptist church with English exiles who later became the Pilgrims of New England. Roger Carey founded one of the first Baptist churches in the American colonies, in Providence, Rhode Island, in 1639.

In common with English Congregationalism (of which the earliest Baptist movement was a wing), the Baptist tradition emphasizes the separation of church and state as well as voluntary church membership. This tradition arose in reaction to the expectation in England that you would just go to the local Church of England church, rather than choosing a church that matched your religious beliefs. Baptists also place prime importance upon their practice of adult baptism . Unlike other denominations, which baptize infants, Baptists baptize only adults, who are old enough to know what they believe and are therefore capable of making a declaration of faith.

Since so many Baptists belong to the Southern Convention, the tradition as a whole has a conservative reputation in many circles. American Baptist churches, however, include some of the most racially diverse and socially liberal congregations you will find in the Bay Area.

FAMOUS FOR: The Baptist baptism is a full immersion rite, in which you are actually dipped or dunked into water, rather than having a few drops sprinkled on you.

OTHER NATIONAL BAPTIST GROUPS: Southern Baptist Convention, National Baptist Convention of America, National Baptist Convention, USA.

WEB SITE: The American Baptist site, www.abc-usa.org, has an adequate congregation search function, as well as a directory of local web sites, which you can search by state and then by city. There are also a host of generic Baptist web sites, with historical essays and many links—the biggest and slickest of these is www.baptist.org.

United Church of Christ

The United Church of Christ (UCC) would not normally be included in a list of the mainline branches of Protestantism, since it is so small. I have included it here because I think many readers of this book might find what they are looking for in a UCC church.

PRIMARY (ONLY) NATIONAL BODY: United Church of Christ, with 1.4 million members nationally.

ANTECEDENTS: Congregational Churches, Reformed Church in the United States, Christian Churches, Evangelical Synod of North America.

HISTORY AND HISTORICAL FIGURES: The UCC was formed in 1957 with the union of the Evangelical and Reformed Church and the Congregational Christian Churches, each of which was itself the product of mergers slightly more than twenty years previously. The Baptist Church and the UCC have a lot of early history in common, especially in the United States—they can both legitimately claim the Pilgrims and Puritans as forebears. Other important historical figures include Anne Hutchinson and Jonathan Edwards.

FAMOUS FOR: The organizing principle of the UCC is "freedom within covenant." The Congregationalist tradition emphasizes the individual congregation and has never been into national hierarchies. There is, therefore, an incredible diversity of practices and opinions, from deeply conservative to radically progressive, among individual UCC churches.

WEB SITE: The national denomination site at www.ucc.org has a wonderful history of the church, including a good history of early Protestantism. The site also has a church locator, through which you can look for congregations by city or by a set radius from your zip code.

Going Church Shopping

So get down upon your knees,

Fiddle with your rosaries,

Bow your head with great respect, and

Genuflect! Genuflect! Genuflect!

—FROM "THE VATICAN RAG" BY TOM LEHRER

After you have thought through your requirements and priorities, come up with a list of prospective churches, and given yourself a terrific pep talk, the armchair phase of your search is complete. Next, you will need to begin the most exciting as well as the most terrifying phase of the whole enterprise, in which you hit the road and actually visit churches. The first outing will probably be the toughest—you might have to mentally yell "Geronimo!" and simply jump in. It gets easier, though; you will come to recognize certain routines that are common to most churches and will feel a lot more comfortable as quickly as your third or fourth outing. You might even find that the first church you visit is the exact right one for you, and never leave.

Phone ahead to double-check the time of the services: all church offices have answering machines or voice mail with an outgoing message that gives the times of the Sunday services, and that message will let you know if there's an extraordinary schedule on a given Sunday or if they've changed their times. You can schedule your visits to fit your inclinations. Some people spend up to a year visiting churches every once in a while, waiting to feel a connection to a given congregation. If for any reason you are on a mission to find a church as expeditiously as possible—if, for example, you have a baby you would like to see baptized, you are engaged and want to be married in a church to which you have some connection, or you've simply made your mind up to get this thing done—you should set aside a string of as many consecutive Sunday mornings as you can. Visit each of the choices on your short list, one after another, for a Sunday morning service. Then go back for a second visit, one after another, to each of the churches that appeals to you.

Some congregations will drop off your list right away, because you have a bad reaction to the pastor or you hate the music or the style of liturgy grates on your nerves. If any of the churches on your prospect list still seem promising after one visit, go back for a second visit—again, one after another. Still more candidates should drop off the list after a second look. If you have any prospects left on your list after you've visited twice, go back a third time. After that third visit, check in with yourself and with anybody else who is searching with you. Have you fallen in love? Does this feel like home? Do you know you've found what you're looking for? If you can't answer an emphatic yes to all of these questions, you should go on looking. Keep any church you haven't written off after three visits on your list of prospects, though. Maybe it is the right place for you and you just need to look around some more before you can know that.

Many people don't find what they're looking for in this first round. You might want to take a week or two off at this point, before you return to your initial list of prospects and pick out three more promising churches. Go through the whole process again—one round of visits, another shorter round, and then a third if need be. If you're not at least falling in like after going through three complete rounds of prospects, you might want to reexamine the assumptions behind your initial selection criteria. Maybe you thought you wanted a big church, but you find yourself feeling a little intimidated or lost. Go visit a few smaller ones to see if that feels better. Perhaps you didn't give a thought to architecture, but when you reflect on your reactions to the churches you've seen you realize that contemporary architecture really leaves you cold. Fine-tuning your search tools might yield a more productive prospect list at this stage.

What you really want to find out about a church is whether or not it's a good fit for you. You might be tempted to dismiss a reaction to a given congregation, either positive or negative, if you can't articulate the reason for it. Don't ignore any strong feelings. Intuition can be your most reliable guide.

Be on the lookout for clues about the church and the people who belong to it. At the point in the service when people stand up and make announcements, pay close attention. You can learn a lot about a church when you know what kinds of activities and concerns people are engaged in. If you're interested in peace and social justice work and all you hear about are rummage sales, you're probably in the wrong place. Look for announcements of outside organizations that people in the church are affiliated with. If there is no mention of alternative sexuality anywhere on a church's bulletin boards or literature, you might not have found the gay-friendly congregation you're looking for. Watch how people treat you as a visitor, and see if it feels good. My church is renowned for its warmth and friendliness toward newcomers. Some people, however, find it overwhelming and are happier in a church with a slightly less gregarious nature.

Be careful to ask some questions before you cross a church off your list, however. I know a couple who moved to San Francisco from New York and visited a church that had been highly recommended by some New York friends who were former parishioners. They found the sermon drab, the music uninspired, and the attendance woefully sparse—they couldn't get out of there fast enough. It took them some time to break the news to their friends that the vibrant church they remembered fondly was a thing of the past. When they did, however, they learned that their visit coincided with a weekend when most of the congregation—including the minister, the music director, the choir, and 95 percent of the parishioners—were away at their annual parish retreat.

Try to find out on your first visit if what you've experienced is typical

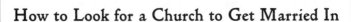

How to Look for a Church to Get Married In

What do you do if you haven't found a church (in fact, truth to tell, you aren't ready yet to look for one), but you are ready to get married? And it needs to be a church wedding, because otherwise your mother will never hear the end of it from her mother, or your future in-laws will fret about what eighty-year-old Aunt Betty from Omaha will think . . . or simply because if it's not a church wedding it somehow won't feel right.

First, you need to find the clergy person who will marry you. Ideally, you will discover someone who is sympathetic, in general terms, to your lifestyle and worldview. This is because most ministers, in order to marry you, will want to spend some time getting to know you and your fiancé. They will have several reasons for this.

To begin with, they feel responsible for making sure that they aren't officiating at a marriage that is an out-and-out disaster waiting to happen. Celebrating the nuptials of every couple that turns up, however ill suited or insincere, would not be a very good thing for the institution of marriage. So most pastors will want to conduct some sort of pre-marriage counseling with both of you, the purpose of which is to be reassured that he or she is doing the right thing by marrying you and to offer you the opportunity, should a serious and previously unrecognized issue surface in the course of this conversation, to improve your chances of making it by resolving the problem before you tie the knot. Some ministers prefer to do multiple sessions readying couples for matrimony, while others want to interview you only once to make sure that the two of you are on the same page vis-à-vis the issues on which most unions falter. The way other clergy cover this territory is to work with you on your wedding vows. You will hear questions like, Have you talked about if and when you will have children? Do you agree about money? How will your relationship change with marriage? (You'd be surprised at what some couples manage to avoid discussing.) Second, most marriage services will include a homily by the pastor, who will want to talk to the assembled guests about the blessings of marriage in general and the joyful occasion of yours in particular. In order for these remarks to be meaningful, the pastor must know a little bit about you, and the best way to learn is to spend a bit of time with you.

You can begin to look for a clergy person to marry you by canvassing your acquaintances. Start by thinking about whether or not you've run across any ministers yourself—in doing community service work, at holiday parties given by the parents of your friends, at other people's weddings. Then ask your friends and colleagues, especially ones who share your values, if they know any clergy. If that doesn't yield any leads, use the church information at the back of this book to find a congregation that seems like a good fit for you. When you have what you think is a good prospect or list of prospects, contact each of them and find out if they perform weddings for people outside their congregation and what the terms are: How much premarital counseling do they require? Do one or both of you have to have been baptized, and does it matter in which denomination? What fees are involved? and so on. Since you are not a member of the congregation, you should expect to pay a rental fee for the use of the church building as well as a fee for the minister's services.

If you know a minister who is ordained but is not the pastor of a congregation, most churches will allow you to rent their sanctuary for a wedding performed by someone else. Many churches have restrictions that prohibit clergy from a different denomination from officiating in the church building, so it will be simplest

continued from page 23

to rent a church of the same denomination as the minister you'd like to have marry you. The minister might even have a church to recommend, such as the congregation where he or she worships or one in which he or she knows the pastor.

When you have found someone you think might be a good fit, try to hear that person preach before you make a final decision. The homily will be a big factor in the emotional tone of your ceremony, and you might decide not to work with someone who you feel is an ineffective speaker.

The search for a minister to perform a same-sex blessing or commitment ceremony would unfold in largely the same way. In quizzing your friends about people they know, of course, you will want to discover very early on the minister's feelings toward gay marriage. If you take the path of calling the pastor at a church you think you might like, contact a church that identifies itself as welcoming, affirming, or inclusive. Even if the regulations of that church's denomination make it impossible to perform a same-sex union in the sanctuary, the minister you speak to will be sympathetic and receptive to your inquiry and might have some good leads for you.

Gay or straight, when you find a clergy person to perform your wedding ceremony, mind your manners—invite him or her to the reception. If he or she has another commitment or would feel awkward attending, you will get a polite refusal. At the end of the day, you might be surprised by how important an element of the whole experience the minister's presence has become. Many couples find that their wedding reception feels somehow incomplete without the presence of the person who guided them in writing their vows, planning their ceremony, and perhaps discovering the full magnitude of what they were doing.

or not. You might want to ask questions such as, Was that your pastor I heard preaching? What is the average Sunday attendance? Is every Sunday service the same? (Some congregations have Eucharist as part of their worship service every other Sunday or once a month, for instance. Many churches periodically have children's services, for which the children forgo Sunday school to remain in the sanctuary.) Is there any regular rotation in the music program? (Some choirs take off a certain Sunday every month; some parishes have monthly guitar masses.) If there are several Sunday services, what are the particular identities of each? (Many congregations have one Sunday service that is smaller and more contemplative and another that is larger and more social. Some churches have services that cater to young singles or to families.)

Of course, this is not the only way to go church shopping. If the prospect of waiting to start church shopping until you've got four to six Sunday mornings in a row free means that you'll wait until next Christmas, by all means break it up. And if you're the type who likes to just jump out of bed one Sunday and drop in on that pretty church you drive past on your way to work every day, even though you know nothing about it, go for it. The key is to get started. It's also very important not to get discouraged if you don't find a good fit right away. As my friend Katy was fond of reminding me during a particularly long boyfriend drought, you only need to get lucky once!

HOW DO I DECIDE WHICH SERVICE TO ATTEND?

Many congregations have more than one service every Sunday morning. In most cases, when there are only two, the later of the two services is the "main" service. The liturgy is often the same at the two services, as is the sermon, but your experiences of the early and the late service at the same church can be very different. The main service, in addition to taking place at a more civilized hour, usually has a few extras—like the choir, church school for children, and nursery care for infants and toddlers—so that attendance is substantially higher.

In big churches that have as many as three or even four Sunday services, each one might have a different focus or style: One is the family service, one the traditional liturgy, one contemporary. You should by all means visit the service that you are more likely to attend on a regular basis. To get the fullest possible picture of the life of a congregation, though, you should make sure that at least one of your visits includes attendance at the "main" service.

WHAT SHOULD I WEAR?

I doubt that any church you are likely to visit in the Bay Area enforces anything resembling a dress code. But if you are, like me, a person who feels a lot less anxious embarking on challenging new experiences when she feels appropriately dressed, I urge you to put together a church-going outfit or two for your exploratory visits.

I recommend erring on the side of caution and dressing as formally as you are comfortable doing on a weekend. Since the emphasis is more on showing respect than on demonstrating how cool you are, church is a setting in which it feels much better to be overdressed than underdressed. When I was church shopping, I would wear the same kinds of clothes I wear to the theater or an evening party. Since I wear jeans for approximately 97 percent of my waking hours, that translated into dressy pants, real shoes (as opposed to sneakers), and a pretty blouse. I also left my lime green polar fleece jacket at home in favor of a black coat.

Once you have settled on a congregation, you will figure out what you want to wear, and in many cases you will settle on something slightly less dressy than your church-shopping ensemble. Of course, if you sport a standard wardrobe regardless of what the people around you look like, do not feel compelled to change your habits. Short of the extreme styles of dress that would attract attention wherever you were, what you wear is unlikely to cause any comment.

GETTING OUT THE DOOR

If you've spent most of the Sunday mornings of your adult life lolling around in your pajamas until noon, you might want to give some thought to strategies for making the experience of getting dressed and out the door on time as pleasant as possible.

It's not much fun—nor is it conducive to either active observation or spiritual calm—to arrive at church, rattled and anxious, five minutes after the service has begun. Not only might you feel awkward and off-balance, but you will also have missed the opportunity to observe what goes on as

Special Considerations for Singles

Uncoupled people can feel some apprehension about visiting churches, expecting not so much to suffer discrimination as to feel like an awkward minority in a family-dominated milieu. The self-evident step might be to gravitate toward congregations, often big ones, that have active singles or young adult groups—and for some people, that choice will be the right one.

Many others, however, ignore the singles factor in their searches. "I moved to San Francisco in 1980 after great experiences with Riverside Church in New York and the Church of the Covenant in Boston. I visited churches when I first moved here, but it took me a couple of years to find the church that felt right," says Cynthia, a straight single woman. "What I was looking for was a church with a challenging liturgy, great preaching, and a community committed to social action. I spent six years at Calvary Presbyterian, but the fact that Calvary had groups for singles and young adults had nothing to do with my choice. On the first Sunday I visited, I heard Bob Conover preach about why AIDS quilts were hanging in the sanctuary, and I made my decision then and there." Cynthia's experience in her church homes has been one of being "welcomed for who I am as an individual, happy to get to know other singles and couples. At my current church, it is a great blessing for me to be part of a community that celebrates and embraces children, who in turn welcome singles as a part of their extended family."

While you won't be rejected for being single by any church you visit or ultimately join, you may bump up against lifestyle differences. John, an uncoupled man in his early thirties, found a compatible congregation that doesn't have a significant number of singles in its membership. "My way of getting to know people is to call them up on the spur of the moment and say, 'Let's go out!' or 'Come over to dinner tonight.' But people with young

continued from page 27

kids don't do well with that kind of invitation, so I have had to be more patient in developing friendships over the course of working with people on the church committees I've joined."

A young adult group can sometimes meet the same needs that a singles group does. John's church, for instance, had nothing for singles but did have a small young adults club. The people in that group, which includes couples as well as singles up to the age of forty, have in common the desire for group outings and spontaneous social activities. Among that collection of people with lifestyles more similar to his own, John is developing friendships on the faster track he's accustomed to, while continuing to cultivate relationships on a slower schedule with others in the congregation.

people wander in and find their seats, and the congregation slowly gathers. So do whatever it takes to ensure that you are able to arrive in moderately good form at church five or ten minutes before the service is scheduled to begin. That probably means getting up a little bit earlier, just to be safe. Maybe it means going out to breakfast, to take some of the sting out of an earlier rising. If you are comatose without caffeine, make sure you've ingested an adequate amount.

WHAT SHOULD I DO WHEN I ARRIVE?

Nearly every church has some sort of system for designating members of the congregation to welcome and assist "visitors" (that's you) and "newcomers" (that will be you when you find a church you want to join). These folks have various titles—ushers or greeters, for instance—and exactly how they handle the job differs from place to place. In some churches they'll just say hello, stick the weekly bulletin or service booklet in your hand, and leave you to your own devices. In other churches they will offer to escort you to a seat. Sometimes they'll ask you if you're a visitor and chat you up a bit. Part of the job of the person who greets you is to answer any questions you might have, so don't hesitate to ask where the bathrooms are, when church school starts, if the pastor is going to preach today, or anything else you want to know.

Once you have settled in your seat, you can start to orient yourself, which is another good reason to arrive a little early. You will often have some sort of printed navigational device available to you. If you weren't handed something at the door, see if there's any kind of small brochure or pamphlet in the pew. This document—a service booklet or weekly bulletin—can help you figure out what's going to happen in the service. Sometimes the weekly bulletin contains the words and music for the entire service. In other cases, the pamphlet will give you an outline for the service and will reference pages for prayers in the prayer book and hymns in the hymnal. Don't panic if you can't find one. Some congregations use bound books only and announce everything you need to know from the pulpit.

Next you should start looking for a prayer book, Bible, and/or hymnal. They are often kept in a pocket or compartment on the back of or below the pew in front of you. If you have a service booklet that tells you where the service is going to start in the prayer book, I think it's a good idea to find that page and bookmark it with the bulletin, so that you don't have to flounder around, flipping through an unfamiliar book, when it's time to begin. (But then again, I pull out my $2 for the bridge toll and stick it in the ashtray before I even turn on the car. You decide how important advance preparation is to you.)

I hate to miss out on even one minute of singing, so I also think it's a good idea to find the first hymn and keep the book open to that page. In many churches, especially ones that don't print up a weekly bulletin, you may notice a small board near the altar or pulpit that has a series of mostly three-digit numbers on it. Chances are good that those are the hymns for the service, listed in the order in which you will sing them. Hymns are usually referred to by the hymn number, not the page number. So if it's hymn 498, don't start flipping through the hymnal looking at the page numbers on the bottom—you should be looking for the hymn number, usually printed in prominent type at the top of the page.

HOW DO I FIGURE OUT WHAT TO DO?

Once the service has begun, you can look to your neighbors for guidance. Not sure which book to pick up? Just look over at the fellow on your left and see what he's doing. The nice thing about being a newbie in church is that the imperative to bring new people in is core to Christian philosophy. Congregations spend a lot of time and energy trying to figure out how they can make visitors welcome. This translates into a genuinely helpful attitude among the folks in the pews, who are more likely to be apologetic for their confusing service than they are to be critical of you for not being able to follow.

Even knowing that, you might still feel particular anxiety about knowing when to sit and when to stand and when to kneel. A general rule of thumb is that you stand to sing, you kneel to pray or be prayed for, and you sit to listen. Exceptions abound, of course—you stand to listen to the Gospel reading, most notably, and some congregations never kneel. The important thing to remember is that nobody cares if you mess up and, in fact, most people won't even notice if you stand up late or you sit when everybody else is sliding into a kneeling position. There are very few churches where everybody knows what to do all the time. Like the hostess at a large and formal dinner party, who picks up the correct utensil with a flourish so that everyone can see which one she's using and copy her, the clergy person officiating at a worship service is ready to be your guide. If you watch for them, you will notice moments in most services when there is a momentary pause, as people hover in indecision (Do we stand for this or sit? What the heck happens next?) and the celebrant hastens to make the move that everyone follows.

A word now about kneelers, those padded planks attached to the pew in front that flip down for kneeling and up to get out of the way when people want to file in or out of the pews. If you are sharing a pew with someone who reaches down to pull the kneeler into action, you can take that as a hint that the next change of body position is likely to involve kneeling. If you activate your own kneeler, make sure that your shins and those of anyone sitting near you are pulled in tight before you pull it down.

ELEMENTS COMMON TO MANY WORSHIP SERVICES

Within a given denomination, most Sunday morning worship services will have the same elements, although they will look radically different in different congregations. A few elements, however, are found in most worship services.

Scripture Readings

Bible readings are included in virtually every worship service, usually at least one from the Old Testament and a Gospel reading from the New Testament. Each denomination has a lectionary, or list of readings for the church year, and in fact there is a Revised Common Lectionary that churches in several denominations use. So it is possible for you go to a Presbyterian church in San Francisco and your mother to her Lutheran church in Pennsylvania and both hear the same Scripture readings.

Sermon or Homily

At some point in the service, someone—probably but not necessarily the pastor—will preach to the congregation, usually on a topic somehow connected to the readings you have just heard. The homily is essentially the congregation's pep talk for the week. The job at hand is figuring out how to be good and caring people in the world, and the sermon is the equivalent of the Monday morning office staff meeting. It is a combination of inspiration that reminds you why you want to be a force for change and tools that help you do a better job of it.

The Passing of God's Peace

Many church worship services, of all denominations, are designed partly to help people get ready for Holy Eucharist, the sacrament in which the people remember the death and resurrection of Christ by eating bread and wine (or grape juice, in some cases) that has been blessed. The definition that the Episcopal Church offers of what getting ready means is one that most churches subscribe to, in one form or another: "It is required that we should examine our lives, repent of our sins, and be in love and charity with all people." Many worship services that don't include Communion are nonetheless designed to help people accomplish these three things.

The Passing of God's Peace, also known as "the Peace," is an opportunity to work on part three of this injunction. During this part of a worship service, the people "greet one another in God's name," to quote the service booklet from my church. This is where people express their love for the members of the Christian community to which they belong, greet strangers (that's you again), and reach out and maybe even make up with any other member of the community with whom they might not be in charity at the moment.

Different congregations handle this part of the service in ways that reflect their individual characters and customs. In one church, people will turn to their immediate neighbors and shake hands, with an exchange of greetings along the lines of "Peace be to you" or "God's peace be with you." At the opposite end of the spectrum are churches in which people roam the aisles to exchange hugs and greetings with most of the people present, in what becomes an extended social break during the service.

As a visitor, you should do whatever it is that makes you comfortable. If you don't feel like offering greetings to your neighbors, wait until they offer them to you. In congregations where members greet one another with physical signs of affection, people are likely to offer to shake your hand, not expecting a stranger to welcome hugs. If words like "God's peace" don't come easily to your tongue, use words that do. "Thank you— to you, too," for instance, is entirely appropriate.

The Offering

At some point during most church services, you will be presented with a collection plate (or basket or some sort of receptacle). If you choose to contribute, put your money in and pass the plate on. But if you happen not to have any small bills, if your experience of the service is enhanced by the feeling that you have been given a gift, or if for any other reason you prefer not to give to the church, you are not under any obligation. After all, this is a church service, not a Mime Troupe performance. The work of the congregation is supported by its members, most of whom pledge a certain amount of money every year and redeem that pledge by putting money in the plate every week or month. If you do want to contribute, your support will be welcome, and checks, made out to the congregation—for example, to "St. John's"—are fine.

Holy Eucharist

Also known as Communion, the Lord's Supper, the Divine Liturgy, the Mass, and the Great Offering, the Holy Eucharist is one of the two sacraments that all mainline Protestant denominations celebrate. Some denominations celebrate Holy Communion with more frequency than others. Most Episcopalian parishes have a Holy Eucharist service every Sunday, whereas Presbyterian and Methodist congregations offer Communion only once a month. Baptism, the other sacrament common to all, is a (Baptism, the other sacrament common to all, is a once-in-a-lifetime event, but Holy Communion is a recurring celebration. The ceremony commemorates the life, death, and resurrection of Jesus Christ and reactivates Christians' sense of their relationship not only to Christ but also to their fellow human beings.

When it comes to "taking" or "receiving" Communion—actually consuming the bread, or bread and wine, or bread and grape juice—churches vary in their methods of distribution. In some parishes, you go up to a Communion rail or station to receive the bread from the hand of ordained clergy and the wine or juice from a minister or a specially trained lay person. In others, members of the congregation remain in their seats and pass the bread and drink to one another. In some places you will be given a hunk of real bread, in others a small wafer; some churches have individual cups of wine or juice, while others pass a communal cup. Many churches change the way they do things periodically, so the pastor might even make an announcement from the altar about where you should go and what you should do to receive Communion.

There is a similar diversity in churches' policies regarding who is eligible to participate. Many churches you visit will welcome any baptized Christian to receive Communion. Others will welcome anybody, baptized or not, and still others offer Communion only to baptized members of their denomination and other sects with which they have established reciprocal cooperative understandings known as full communion.

Churches generally state their policies, both in an announcement from the altar by the pastor and in the printed service booklet. Sometimes the language is a tad ornate, so you should keep your ears open for keywords. If you hear something that begins with "This table does not belong to us alone" and includes phrases like "all God's children"—as opposed to "all

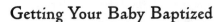

Getting Your Baby Baptized

There are certain conditions, mostly having to do with cultural traditions and family pressures, under which you might find yourself wanting to have your child baptized, even though you yourself haven't yet found or aren't ready to join a faith community. What you really want is a church with which you can have a short-term and frankly cold-blooded relationship. This quest, while not unlike that of looking for a church for your wedding, is a tricky proposition.

Baptism, after all, is an initiation into the Christian community, and infant baptism presumes that the parents and the caring adults who stand as godparents will transmit their Christian values to the child. So it's not really in line with the meaning of the whole ritual to abruptly appear someplace you've never been, with the evident intention of never showing up again, and ask people with whom you have no relationship, "Hey, would you mind baptizing my kid so that my mother will get off my back?" This is not to say, however, that it can't be done.

The path of least resistance is to have your baby baptized in the denomination in which you grew up. (I'm assuming here that one of the parents involved did grow up going to church—otherwise, where would the pressure be coming from?) Your home parish will have records of your baptism and confirmation and so on, which the local church you approach might need to get hold of. A Lutheran parish secretary is going to find it a whole lot easier to locate and talk to your Lutheran parish in your hometown than with a Methodist secretary. There is also a sense of hope in all traditions that those who grew up in the faith will one day return to it, and baptizing your child could possibly be the first step down that road.

You could think about having your baby baptized in the congregation you grew up in, especially if your parents are still members. That's an obvious solution for cases in which the grandparents are local, but you might even consider it if the parents or in-laws in question live far away. My sister, for instance, travels from Arizona every summer to bring her children on a visit to their grandparents in New Jersey. She wasn't attending any church regularly when her daughters were born, so during the summer visits she asked my mother to help her set up baptisms in the parish we belonged to as children.

If neither of these scenarios is an option, you can look for a local church. You will probably find that congregations that are more oriented toward being inclusive and welcoming—the churches described in Chapters 5 and 6 as friendly to gays and cultural creatives, for example—will be most willing to help you out. (But don't forget that Baptists don't do infant baptisms.) You should be prepared to attend baptism preparation sessions with the pastor and to be open about your reasons for wanting to have your child baptized even though you don't go to church yourself. I don't mean to suggest that the minister will give you a hard time about not going to church, merely that he or she will want to determine that you are sufficiently respectful of the sacrament, which is a significant event for the church community.

Whatever the reasons driving you to have your baby baptized, don't neglect one of the most delightful aspects of the whole experience: choosing godparents who will sponsor your child for baptism, which essentially amounts to picking out an adult (other than his or her parents, who will quickly be taken for granted) from whom your child will always receive special attention. Most parents choose friends who are willing and able to be a caring presence in their child's life and whose values they share. Practices vary among denominations concerning how many sponsors one

continued from page 35

child can have and whether the sponsors must have any qualifica-
tions—for example, they themselves might have to be baptized
Christians. The clergy person you're working with can fill you in
on all the rules and recommendations and can even help with any
unusual wrinkles. It is possible, for example, to have someone
who is not able to attend the ceremony stand as a godparent by
proxy, so that your child can have as a godparent a friend who is
temporarily living far away.

baptized Christians"—they are saying that everyone is invited. If, however,
you hear or read anything about "close" or "closed" Communion or even
"baptized faithful," they are most likely not talking about you.

You should understand, however, that a church's policy is driven by theological concerns, not mean-spiritedness. The variety in policies arises from
differing interpretations of how much shared belief is necessary among participants in Communion. Even if you were to make a mistake and present
yourself at the altar rail in a congregation that offers Communion only to
members of their own faith, the pastor would consider your feelings very
carefully in choosing how to deal with the situation.

If you do meet the eligibility requirements of a church you are visiting,
don't be shy about receiving Communion if you'd like to. Even if you feel
slightly at sea, it's not a very complicated ritual. Generally, the bread and
wine are offered to everyone in the same fashion, so you will have an opportunity to observe others before it's your turn. Often, whoever presents the
gifts speaks a phrase, to which there is a brief response. If you can't catch
what the people ahead of you have said, that's fine. "Amen" is generally a safe
fallback, and no one would be unduly fazed if you said nothing.

For one reason or another, you may not want to take wine if that's
what is offered. You are not alone in that preference, and the person giving it out will be sensitive to any gesture you make that indicates refusal.
Many people choose to cross their hands over their chests and bow their
heads briefly to indicate that they'd like to pass up the wine; sometimes a

minister will choose to briefly touch your head and bestow a blessing if you don't take the wine.

CLUES THAT TELL YOU WHAT YOU WANT TO KNOW

Whenever you visit a church, look around for clues as to what kind of community it is and how well it matches up with what you are looking for. You can detect a number of things about a congregation from the way in which its members come together for the worship service, for instance. Is it a bustling environment, in which people stop to chat and visit on their way to a seat? Or is the atmosphere more hushed, with the majority of the parishioners seeming to prefer the solitude of their own thoughts? Depending on what you're looking for in a worship experience, you might prefer one style over the other.

How are you treated as a visitor? This is an area in which one man's meat is another's poison. You might be delighted to have a member of the church you're visiting take you by the hand and sit with you, at the ready with instructions and guidance. I might find it suffocating, however, and would be delighted with the more hands-off treatment at another church, in which you felt sorely neglected. Were you moved and engaged by the sermon? Did the preacher (don't forget to ascertain whether or not it was the pastor) make anybody laugh? Did she or he use a vocabulary you could relate to?

If there is a weekly bulletin, you will want to mine that for all kinds of information about the church community. There should be a schedule of services and announcements of activities for the week. This can give you a picture of the kinds of groups and activities the church itself has, as well as the sorts of outside activities people in the church are engaged in. Announcement time, during which people generally go up to the front of the church and make announcements that are of interest to others, should be a similar treasure trove of information about the inner life of the parish.

HOW YOU ARE LIKELY TO BE WELCOMED

In addition to the individuals whose job it is to greet everyone who shows up for church on a Sunday morning, most congregations have an additional group of people who focus on following up with visitors. Some of these folks, who are often called something like the welcome team or the evangelism committee (that's one of those buzzwords that means something perfectly unobjectionable, honest), might approach you after the worship service and ask you some questions and invite you to do several things.

These conversations will often open with the question of whether you are a visitor. (The answer is yes.) The next question will probably be, "Are you from the area or visiting from out of town?" When you say you're local, the person will likely ask if you are church shopping. If you've pretty much written a church off and are really interested in skulking out the door as quickly and quietly as possible, you can make a graceful exit at this point. Announce that you've just begun your search and that you have a list of churches you're looking forward to visiting. You can politely refuse if you're asked to sign a welcome book or visitors' register.

If you think you might still be interested, take advantage of any overtures you receive to find out as much as possible about a potential church. Sign the welcome book, so that they know where to send the information that's distributed to prospective members. When someone volunteers to introduce you to the pastor, accept their offer. If you're interested in singing in the choir, ask to meet the music director. Make sure you meet the youth minister or the director of the Sunday school if you have children.

Almost every church has some kind of short social gathering after the main Sunday service. Known most commonly as the "coffee hour" or "fellowship," it is essentially a cocktail party without booze. People stand around, clutching coffee cups instead of wine glasses and balancing small plates of food. From the conversations you will have—typical cocktail party chat, like "What do you do?" "Where do you live?" "Where do your children go to school?" "What brings you here today?"—you can gather information about who people are and where they come from. Not unlike surviving an earthquake, the experience of church shopping is one that many people love to relive by telling their own stories every chance they get. Ask the folks you meet how long they've been members of this particular church and what drew them to it. Often, people's responses will have a pattern that can identify the particular strengths and priorities of a given congregation for you.

File away all the information you gather, impressions and hard data alike, from your first visit to a church that you think you might consider joining. When you go back for a second visit, double-check to make sure that you have built an accurate picture. If you experience a strong emotional attraction to a particular church, review how closely it meets your original set of criteria. If it doesn't and you are contemplating throwing over those priorities, review the reasons why you established them in the first place and think about whether you can do without them.

After all, it is unlikely that you will find every single thing you want and need in one place. You might find a congregation that, on paper, has everything you require, but the experience of being there leaves you cold. It's equally possible that you could visit a church that is not a complete match with your requirements, but the worship services are the most exciting spiritual experiences you've had in recent memory.

You might discover that the priorities you identified from your armchair are overthrown by what you learn about your desires and needs in real experiences of church. When you find a church that, after three visits, appears to fulfill your requirements, seems like a place you'd look forward to coming to at least once a week, and feels like a community you want to commit to, your shopping days are over.

Making a Commitment

It is madness to wear ladies' . . . hats to church; we should all be wearing crash helmets. Ushers should issue life preservers and signal flares; they should lash us to our pews. For the sleeping God may wake someday and take offense, or the waking God may draw us out to where we can never return.

—FROM *Teaching a Stone to Talk* BY ANNIE DILLARD

In many ways, the experience of finding a church home and creating a space for it in your life is like finding true love. Different people have different relationships with their churches. I was never cut out to be a wild single woman and I found that I pretty quickly wanted to go steady with my church, too. But some people date their churches for many months or even years. They go through spates of regular attendance at services, then drop out for long periods of time; they might throw something generous into the collection plate every time it passes them, but they never promise ahead of time to contribute a certain sum over the course of the year; or they are regular in their attendance and financial support, but they hold back from completing whatever formal mechanism the church requires for official membership. For a long time after I started taking a turn as a greeter at my church, I hesitated to ask people I didn't recognize if they were newcomers. I had once too often gotten the affronted response of "I've been coming here for twenty years!" from someone who omitted to tell me that his schedule of attendance was on the order of once a quarter over that period of time.

Other folks might find the right church but at the wrong time. Several years ago, a couple with a ten-month-old girl started coming to St. Aidan's quite regularly. I chatted with them whenever I saw them at coffee hour and found out that they were new to the area and liked the church a lot. At some point they stopped coming, only to reappear almost a year later, at which point I began to see them every Sunday once again. It turned out that coming to a 10:00 a.m. service meant the baby missed her morning nap, which made her unbearably grouchy for the rest of the day. The parents decided that coming to church wasn't worth a miserable Sunday every week, so they stayed away until their daughter was old enough to drop her morning nap. And then there's the case of my friend Pat, who found a truly compatible church in the second congregation she visited. Her husband had no interest in joining her, however, and she soon came to see that by going to church for two hours on Sundays she was losing one of the few times during the week that she and Matthew regularly had time to themselves. Given the toll their high-pressure jobs were already exacting on their marriage, she decided to forgo Sunday morning services until life calmed down a bit.

I will confess here to a heavy prejudice in favor of making the maximum commitment that your life can accommodate to the church you choose. I know—because I have experienced it more than once—that everything you put into communities like schools and neighborhood groups and churches comes back to you multiplied by ten. And I'm not talking about any ethereal, after-worldly kind of benefits, either. What you will gain are the instant-gratification variety of joys that are to be had when you commit yourself to a group of people, when you put your shoulder to the wheel alongside them and try to do some good in the world together, when you have a community in which you can both celebrate and mourn with equal abandon.

That said, I can also vouch for the fact that many people have happy relationships that look nothing like mine. Just as the process of looking for a church can take a variety of forms that appear nowhere on the suspiciously neat map I've laid out in the previous two chapters, the connection you build with the church you select will follow its own path. While the demands of your life and your own spiritual needs will be the most important factors, it can be helpful to have a sense of the most common patterns other people choose.

OPTIONS FOR BUILDING CHURCH INTO YOUR LIFE

What follow are descriptions of the three most common types of relationships people form with their churches. The subjects of my field study in this department were both the people I have seen coming and going (and coming again) in my own church community and my friends and acquaintances who are in the process of building church into their lives.

Permanent Visitor

Some people simply never join the congregation they've selected as their church home. Many of the individuals I've encountered who fall into this category are quite clear about their reasons for worshiping regularly in one place yet holding back from actually signing up. Some go so far as to cultivate relationships with members of the congregation; others show up only occasionally for worship services and don't get involved with anybody or anything else.

My neighbor Joanne, for example, goes to Sunday services at her friend Mary's Unitarian church almost every week. Although she has been doing this for more than five years, and the total of what she gives to the collection plate in a year is a substantial amount of money, she refuses to either make a financial commitment to the church or to be formally included in any way in the rolls of the congregation. She has made some friends in the congregation, and since her retirement last year she has been logging many volunteer hours every week in church-sponsored community service activities, yet she has steered clear of joining any committees. Why would this seemingly typical church lady be so resolute in her refusal to fully embrace the congregation that evidently means so much to her? Joanne is a first-generation Italian-American married to a man with the same background. Between them, she and Sal number two priests and three nuns among their siblings alone—they're not sure what the total count is if you include aunts, uncles, and cousins. Neither of them is willing to take on the scandal they are confident would erupt if the families learned that Joanne had left the Catholic Church, which no longer fulfills her particular spiritual needs. So the solution she has contrived is to worship and do community service with the Unitarians but to shy away from any formal membership, so that she technically remains a member of the parish church Sal continues to attend on his own.

I have another friend who is a permanent visitor for a different yet equally compelling set of reasons. Pam has been worshiping in the same church for three or four years, but she, like Joanne, has never joined. Pam will attend the main Sunday service every week for a considerable length of time, yet when her caseload as a hospice counselor becomes uncomfortably heavy she drops out abruptly, and no one sees her for months. Pam has avoided joining the church because the freedom to disappear at will is important to her. She is also wise enough to recognize that she has a specific set of spiritual needs that the Sunday worship service addresses adequately. Her life, already overfull with a consuming job and graduate studies, cannot accommodate any more friendships or any more commitments, however light. Even though nobody takes attendance at church and no mandated level of involvement is attached to membership, Pam knows that she herself would feel the need to let people know where she was and to sign up for something if she actually joined the church. She finds that the status of permanent visitor is the most comfortable and stress-free choice for her at this point in her life.

For reasons like these, or others of your own—you can't quite get your head around the idea of actually joining a church, you are living somewhere temporarily, you are moving through what you know will be a short-term phase of your spiritual quest—you might consider the status of permanent visitor.

Dual Allegiance

Some people find themselves belonging, either as full members or as permanent visitors, to two different congregations. They do this for a variety of reasons: Some folks have country houses and city apartments, some people's jobs demand that they split their time between two different states, and some people live in one place but desire the mixture of experiences that membership in a cathedral congregation as well as in a parish church offers. Some people even belong to two faith communities of different religious traditions: adult children of interfaith marriages belong to both a Christian church and a Jewish temple, or people belong to a Zen center for their own practice and join a Western church with their children.

If there are circumstances in your life that make it difficult to find a single church home that meets all your needs, you might want to consider dual membership. Although it might seem like a recipe for disastrous overextension, when you have consciously chosen this type of arrangement with a clear idea of the separate roles you expect your two faith communities to play in your life, you can make it work quite well.

Full Membership

On the face of it, full membership in a church might not seem like a good idea. It certainly flies in the face of the advice we are given everywhere we turn—in magazine articles, newspaper stories, and television specials—on how to manage stress, the number-one evil of contemporary life. We're supposed to be reducing the number of commitments in our lives, not increasing them!

When you visit a church on Sunday mornings, it's a bit like being a guest at a party. Your hosts have cleaned the place up and decorated nicely. They put on a program of music and readings that's both entertaining and thought provoking, and they serve you a meal. As a guest, you sit back, enjoy everything that's presented to you, and maybe even marvel at how well done it all is. You might even choose to be a permanent visitor if that experience is exactly what you want and is adequate to your spiritual needs.

After you have been going to a church regularly for a while and you've started to make friends and participate in parish social activities, however, at some point someone will invite you to join in the behind-the-scenes work that goes into the party the church hosts every week. The choice is entirely up to you, and people will understand if you say no. But if you are able to come behind the curtain screening the kitchen from the party guests, you will find a wealth of rewards in deepened connections to other people and the satisfactions of making a contribution. When you join one of the committees or work groups that drive the various programs of a church, you make your own contribution to the activities that you, your family, and the world at large all benefit from. It's also the best way to integrate yourself into a community. Think about how long it's going to take you to get to know people if the only contact you have is ten minutes of chitchat once a week after the church service. Then consider how your acquaintance with someone might develop if you spent several hours together every few weeks working out the Sunday school plans for the year or organizing the meals for the homeless program.

Full membership means getting involved to the fullest extent that you can. When you have visited a church a few times, you will begin to get a sense of what it looks like to really belong as you observe the folks who already do. First of all, they're the people you see every time you go, because they go to church unless something specific comes up that prevents them from doing so. You will also notice that they have a sense of ownership of the place. If there's a pool of water on the floor inside the front door because it's raining cats and dogs, two or three people will take it upon themselves to go find a mop, rather than just watching the puddle grow because it's not their job to fix it. Finally, they are the ones who seem to have really close friends in the church community. In the course of one of those idle coffee hour chats, you will hear from the woman you're talking to that the college student across the room is her goddaughter and they've gone on a backpacking trip together every year since the girl was ten, that the two women with whom you've been exchanging Weight Watchers war stories have been walking together every weekday morning for more than twenty years, that the mother of the twin toddler boys playing in the corner had dinner delivered to her door every day while she was on bed rest for the final three months of her pregnancy.

HOW YOU CAN OFFICIALLY JOIN

When you have settled on the congregation that you want to have as your church home, you should register in some fashion. You don't have to wait until you've decided how committed you want to be. As soon as you know that you've finished shopping, you're ready. Most congregations have devised a set process to welcome newcomers, a checklist of opportunities for you to learn more about the congregation and how it operates and for the clergy and possibly some lay leaders to learn more about you and your spiritual needs. Don't worry, though—in most churches you are given a great deal of latitude to decide which things you want to do and which you don't. If you don't take Communion and you intend to remain an uninvolved permanent visitor, flying beneath the radar of official membership records, you don't have to do anything, strictly speaking. It's only courteous, however, to at least let the clergy person in charge know who you are and what you're up to. If you don't, if you just keep showing up on Sunday mornings, the minister and the lay people on the welcome committee— who keep tabs on how newcomers are shepherded through the process of joining the church—will end up thinking, every time they look at you, "Hey! We must have screwed up. How'd we miss that one?"

You will be invited to kick off the welcome process. In smaller congregations, someone will approach you after you've signed the welcome book (or whatever apparatus your particular congregation uses to keep track of visitors who might become members) and shown up at Sunday worship services several times. Some larger congregations distribute forms in the pews or at the door of the church, which you fill out to let the church know that you want to get started. Although a certain amount of variety exists in the systems different churches use for inviting people to join, they are universally user-friendly and, aside from that first indication of interest, won't require any initiative on your part.

Interview with the Minister

One of the earliest things you will do is have a face-to-face meeting with the chief clergy person in charge of the congregation. In some rare cases of very large churches in which the volume of both pastoral duties and newcomers is enormous, this duty is delegated to assistant pastors. You and the minister arrange your meeting for a time and place that's comfortable and convenient for you. One minister might like to visit you in your home; another might invite you to his or her office or to go out for coffee or lunch.

This meeting has a number of purposes. It allows you to begin to develop a personal rapport with the minister, and it allows the minister to get a sense of who you are and what you are seeking in the church community. This is your chance, if you want to participate very lightly, to let the clergy person know your intentions. If you have a well-developed sense of your spiritual path and you like to talk about it, this would be a good chance to share that information. Talk about your doubts if you are unsure of what you believe, both to let the pastor know you more and to see how he or she reacts. If you suffer from any chronic health problems, recent bereavements, or family problems for which you might be needing counseling from the minister, you could share that in this interview. The pastor, in turn, can let you know about what the church has to offer that seems most pertinent to your particular circumstances—adult education courses, grief support groups, or quiet prayer services, for instance.

Or you could do none of these things and just have the kind of general get-acquainted chat you might have with a new neighbor. When David and I first joined St. Aidan's, I was horrified when David told me he had arranged for the priest, Jim, to come visit us one evening. In the church I grew up in, the parish priest would come to the house only when someone had died or been arrested (the latter of which never happened in my family, my mother would want me to add). Perhaps because the only exposure I'd ever had to the rector-coming-to-visit situation was in the pages of Jane Austen and Barbara Pym, I decided to serve tea when our priest came to see us. My only memories of that visit are of me spilling the contents of the teapot all over the living room floor and of Rosie, a two-year-old at the time, dirtying her diaper as she sat in Jim's lap. Even if I'd been capable of articulating anything sensible about my spiritual path at the time, which I wasn't, I doubt we would have gotten around to it. Both David and I felt that we knew Jim somewhat better after that chat, however, and if a crisis in our lives had driven us to go to him for help it would have been a lot easier to do so because of his visit.

A Brief Overview of Prerequisites to Membership

LUTHERAN: This denomination practices open Communion, so Evangelical Lutheran Church in America (ELCA) churches offer Communion to all baptized Christians. If you want to join an ELCA congregation, you will be asked to attend a new members class, after which you will be received into the church during a brief ritual incorporated into a worship service.

PRESBYTERIAN: To join a Presbyterian church, you will need to take a new-members class. At the end of your period of instruction, you will be asked to go first before the session of elders, the governing body of your individual congregation, and then before the entire congregation, in a public ritual profession of your faith, in which you basically say out loud that you subscribe to certain core beliefs. This ceremony of reception into the church is not designed to expose nonbelievers, however; no one will quiz you on how deeply or how literally you believe. Presbyterians also include all baptized Christians—some congregations even welcome all "sincere believers"—to Communion.

METHODIST: Methodists offer Communion to anybody, but they're pretty clear that since it is a Christian ritual, they're going to encourage you to get baptized if you want to do it on a regular basis. If you have been baptized but never confirmed, you will be asked to prepare for a public affirmation of your baptismal vows on your way to being received as a member of the Methodist Church. You will also be asked, in the course of that ceremony, to pledge your loyalty to the United Methodist Church (UMC) and to promise to support your individual congregation. If you have been baptized and confirmed in a denomination that allows you to transfer your membership to the UMC, that's all you have to do.

continued from page 49

EPISCOPAL: All Episcopal churches offer Communion to anyone who's been baptized, and many offer it to everyone. New members or inquirers classes are offered to people who are new to the Episcopal Church, and you can officially join by transferring your membership from the denomination in which you were baptized or confirmed (if they allow that) and being received into the Episopcal Church. If you were baptized but never confirmed, you will no doubt be encouraged to go ahead with a confirmation class and to ultimately be confirmed.

BAPTIST: Baptists have such a strong tradition of congregational independence that there is a great variety within the practices of individual churches when it comes to membership. You will certainly be encouraged to be baptized if you have not yet been, although American Baptist churches will offer Communion (which they don't have too often, maybe once a month) to anyone who wants it.

UNITED CHURCH OF CHRIST: United Church of Christ churches are also oriented to the primacy and independence of the individual congregation. They have an equally strong traditional belief in the notion that your belief is private, so it is unlikely that you will be asked to make any public professions of faith.

Pledging Financial Support

Often your minister will talk to you about making a financial commitment to the church during the course of your welcome visit, but he won't ask you for money. His remarks will focus on the spiritual aspects of stewardship and the responsibility of members to support the work of the church. In many congregations the solicitation and tracking of financial support for members is handled entirely by lay people. In my church, for instance, the rector deliberately remains ignorant of exactly how much anyone gives to the church and, in fact, which people are making contributions on a regular basis and which aren't.

Someone from the congregation will talk to you about promising to contribute money to the church on a regular basis. You choose the amount you want to give and you make a promise or pledge to give that amount of money, on a schedule—weekly, monthly, quarterly, or yearly—that works for you. You redeem your pledge, or fulfill your promise, by putting checks in the collection plate for the appropriate amount on the schedule you've committed to throughout the year.

There is generally a committee of lay people whose job it is to encourage people to contribute money to the church. They organize an annual fund drive, or stewardship campaign, once a year, during which you will be asked to think about your contributions to the church and fill out a pledge card for the coming year. If you join the church, as most of us do, outside the time frame of this annual fundraising drive, you won't be given the full stewardship treatment until the next cycle. Some churches operate in much the same way that Stanford and the symphony approach potential donors, and will send someone from the stewardship committee to visit you and talk to you about the finances of the church, how much money the congregation gives every year, and so on. Other churches are more casual in their approach with newcomers. At St. Aidan's, I think someone handed David a pledge card at coffee hour one Sunday and asked him to hand it in to the church office when he had a chance.

You might hear a sermon about stewardship at some point while all this is going on. Before I had actually heard one, the very idea of a preacher talking about giving money utterly horrified me. To begin with, muddying the spirituality of a worship service with the business of money seemed cynical and somehow sleazy. I also had the vague expectation of being brutally exhorted to give away everything I owned or at least to donate one-tenth of my income to the church. Of course, there was nothing in my experience of the church I joined to support these expectations—they were half-baked prejudices derived from cultural myths about money-grubbing parsons. As it turns out, there are theological aspects to this business of giving money to the church that make it an absolutely appropriate sermon topic. Some of the related ideas, such as abundance, are even radical and liberating.

Despite the wide variety in the approaches they take, all churches share a delicacy and sensitivity in their stewardship efforts. They are much more interested in having you make the commitment of a pledge than they are in the amount you contribute. You need not fear that you will feel pressured or embarrassed.

Prerequisites to Joining a Church

Churches vary widely in what they require of newcomers vis-à-vis formal membership. If all you want to do is show up at services and sit in the pew and pray and sing, nobody can require you to do anything. But if you want to receive Communion and serve on certain governance committees—if you want to participate fully in the worship and community life of the congregation, in other words—you may have to take a Christian education course and/or take part in a ritual or two.

Even the most casual and inclusive churches tend to think that it's important for you to have been baptized. The importance vested in this rite of initiation stems from the essential idea of what it means to be a Christian. The relationship among the individual, God, and the community is a committed kinship with both rights and responsibilities flowing among all the parties involved. Baptism is the route by which you enter this covenant. Thus, in a great many churches baptism is a prerequisite for taking Communion, which is in part a celebration of the oneness among all Christians.

For some denominations, it's enough to have been baptized, regardless of the church in which it was done. Others, however, observe what is known as "closed Communion." The theology of their tradition dictates that Communion can be the profound experience it's meant to be only when all who partake of it are sufficiently close in belief as to be members of their denomination or others with whom they have worked out agreements to be in "close communion" with. For example, if you found a Lutheran church you really liked that was part of the Lutheran Church–Missouri Synod (LCMS), and you were at one time baptized in the Episcopal Church, with which the LCMS is not in close communion, you would not receive Communion. You would wait until you had completed a membership class, in which you would learn about LCMS doctrine, and then be inducted as an LCMS member, at which time you would be eligible to receive Communion.

If you've never been baptized and you're serious about this church business, at some point you will probably choose to be baptized. As an adult preparing for baptism, you will be required to take some form of instruction in the faith tradition you've chosen. This won't be a course in what you should or must believe, however—it will be more of an orientation to the meaning of baptism and the implications of being a Christian. For many people who are baptized as adults, the actual ceremony is often the culmination of an intense period of inquiry and growth and a touchstone experience in their spiritual journeys.

Congregations are very clear and up-front about what you need to do if you want to join. When you have your welcome interview with the minister, he or she will ask you about your religious background and will no doubt fill you in on what you'll have to do, if anything, to officially join the church. Some churches require baptized Christians of other denominations to take an adult education course on the history and beliefs of their tradition and to take part in some sort of ceremony. You needn't feel that you have to stop coming to church until you've gone through the course, however. You just have to be sensitive about hanging back from those things, like receiving Communion, that your church restricts.

Transfer of Documents
Another element in the process of joining a church is paperwork. Some congregations think it's important to have written documentation of your religious history, while others embrace a far more casual attitude. If you are joining a church in the same denomination in which you were baptized or confirmed, it's a relatively simple matter for the parish administrator to request that the parish in which you received those sacraments transfer your records to your new church home, in a procedure that's not unlike requesting a copy of your school transcript. You might need to call or write your old church (especially if it's been a while) to ask that a copy of your records be forwarded if you are coming from a different denomination. You could easily slip out of this job, however, if the prospect is distasteful to you.

FURTHER ON DOWN THE LINE

After you have done whatever it takes to join your new church, the next step (which will take some time) is to make a place for yourself in the church and to make a place in your life for the church.

When I first joined my church, I would see a mass of unknown or vaguely familiar faces every Sunday when I went into the Sunday morning service. In the context of worship, this experience was just fine and perfectly comfortable. I was eager to experience the sense of community I felt so strongly at St. Aidan's, however. Many people would chat me up every week at coffee hour, but I found that my acquaintance with any one person didn't advance much during a series of short conversations spread over a number of weeks. It was only when I found some smaller groups to be part of that I began to develop the friendships with people that so greatly enrich my experience of the church. These smaller groups can be either social/educational or service oriented. I first got to know people by taking a few adult education courses and then made some really warm friendships when I joined the team of Sunday school teachers. I think it's just fine to be strategic and focused on your own needs in this search for small groups, especially at first.

Most congregations have social or support groups organized along various affinity lines—men's groups, singles groups, young adult groups, parenting groups, women's groups, and so on. When you are new, it is especially easy to shop around, trying out a few groups before making the choice of which one will do the best job for you. If you are leery of adding another monthly meeting to your schedule, you might prefer to try small groups of limited duration, like an adult education series or the small-dinner groups that some churches arrange for newcomers. Whichever small-group situation you choose, your goal is to find people you think you might want for friends and get to know them better.

Making a place in your life for your church means not only making the time to show up regularly on Sunday mornings, it also means finding the capacity, emotionally as well as temporally, to be a part of the community and to contribute to its work. Again, you can go as slowly as you need to on this front. Don't feel compelled to take on more than you can handle or to do something you don't want to simply because you have been asked.

When you do begin to join in, serving on a committee or two and pitching in on projects here and there, your church work may become one of the most rewarding aspects, both socially and spiritually, of your life.

I can imagine that you might find the thought of all this involvement a bit overwhelming as you read about it here. You are thinking about church in the first place because you want more peace and sanity in your life, right? If you can't quite picture how you'll manage to squeeze even a few hours from your life to go to church once a week, the prospect of signing away hours and hours to classes or committee meetings must seem like a particularly stupid step in the wrong direction. It seems especially insane when you have nothing concrete—no specific community of people you know and like—to imagine making this kind of commitment to. Fortunately, you will find that the process of weaving the church into your life is a gradual and willing one. Taking on activities that replenish you is a different proposition from accepting responsibilities that exhaust you. When you leave a church dinner or an evening class filled with more joyful energy than you had coming in, you will be eager to say yes to the next invitation that comes your way.

PART TWO

Specific advice on finding a church for
families with young children; lesbians,
gays, bisexuals, and transgendered individuals;
spiritual seekers, cultural creatives,
and political progressives

Finding a Church
for the Whole Family

Often parents ask how to bring their children to God,
but I like to speak first about how children bring us to God.

—FROM *Whole Child, Whole Parent* BY POLLY BERRIEN BERENDS

How tough can it be to find a church for the kids? I certainly thought it would be a simple matter to track down a few churches that "specialized" in children, check them out, and pick the one I liked the best. Guess what? All churches love children. Even congregations that aren't especially fond of actually seeing or hearing them too often will tell you— and in fact believe themselves—that they love kids. And among parishes that love the fact as well as the theory of young ones, there is considerable variety in the ways in which that love is shown. Some of the differences are a function of size, some are a function of theology. There are pluses and minuses attached to each of these styles; you need to consider the possibilities and make a choice based on your own values and preferences.

Many parents start their searches thinking that the best choice for them will be the church that has the biggest Sunday school program they can find, with gleaming nurseries, shiny new toys, and loads of children being taught by a huge corps of teachers. Large church school programs, which are most often attached to large churches, often have enviable resources, such as full-time ordained youth ministers, a well-trained lay teaching staff, and funds for supplies. They can also offer opportunities for kids that require a critical mass of children the same age, such as junior choirs, grade-specific curricula, and an ample pool of potential buddies that are the right age and gender.

At first glance, you might think there's no contest between that kind of situation and another congregation that has no Sunday school program at all. That church with no separate facility for kids, however, might be one of the parishes that have made loving children such a central part of their identity that they don't send the children off to Sunday school while the adults hang out in church together. They have made the radical commitment to accept children as full members of their community, which means that they worship in a way that allows the children to be present and to participate in the whole of the service. (Everybody goes to Sunday school together, too.) That experience has an entirely different set of riches to offer your family.

SIGNS OF A KID-FRIENDLY CULTURE

Kid-friendly churches are comfortable having children around, even when the little dears aren't at their best. When you go on exploratory visits to Sunday morning services, be on the lookout for signs of how comfortable the adults in the congregation are with having children—including children who are being noisy or obnoxious—join them in worship.

If you bring your child on an exploratory visit, he or she might not want to go off to Sunday school with a bunch of strangers. If the greeter or usher pushes the Sunday school option so assiduously that you end up feeling funny about having your kid stay with you, it's probably not a kid-friendly church. Try to sit near a babe in arms during the service and watch what

What's the Difference Between Children and Youth? And Other Mysteries Explained

When I first started looking at churches and talking to people about programs for kids, my head would spin as I tried to keep track of what the heck everybody was talking about. Having eventually figured it out, I am happy to share my hard-won knowledge with you. May you never feel as dizzy as I once did.

NURSERY CARE generally means babysitting for infants and toddlers, as opposed to SUNDAY SCHOOL, which refers to an actual program of instruction, usually for children of preschool age and older. YOUTH will often be applied as a generic term to all young people, as in "What does the church offer our youth?" and grand questions along those lines. It is also used more specifically for a particular age group when you hear people making a distinction between children and youth. In those cases, depending on the particular church, the "youth" are teenagers or sometimes preteens as well as adolescents.

CHURCH SCHOOL is a term that's pretty much interchangeable with SUNDAY SCHOOL; it simply accommodates the fact that some churches hold church school classes at a time other than Sunday morning. CHRISTIAN EDUCATION embraces programs for adults as well as children and youth. Some congregations have a Christian education minister rather than a youth minister; that person's job is usually more than half dedicated to children and youth, however.

Elementary school children usually come to church because their parents bring them. Church school programs for them are designed to teach them some Bible stories, to develop a sense of God and of the church community, and to allow them to have some fun together so that they like coming to church. Most often, church school for young children does happen on Sunday morning,

continued from page 61

whether or not it overlaps with the main worship service.

Once your children are old enough to be classified as youth, you will notice a change in their Christian education. The people running the youth programs are no fools. They realize (maybe even before you do!) that when children reach adolescence they are not only old enough to stay home alone, they are also at the exact right age for making their parents' Sunday morning a living hell if they are dragged, unwilling, to church. Most YOUTH PRO-GRAMS, in addition to Christian education, include an element called something like "youth group" or "teen fellowship." This set of activities might include educational or adventure outings with the youth minister or adult members of the congregation; social evenings at the church, to which kids are encouraged to invite their other friends outside the church; community service activities, such as serving at a soup kitchen; and regularly scheduled unstructured hang-around time, like a weekly study hall at the church. The name of the game here is to build up the social friendships among a cohort of preteens or teenagers so that, like the little kids playing together in Sunday school, they like to come to church.

happens when the baby cries or fusses. Do you sense a lot of tension in the people around you, as if they're waiting anxiously for the noise to go away so that they can get on with it? Or do you notice people sending the mother supportive glances that clearly say, "I love hearing a baby"? (Well maybe that's a lot to ask. How about, "Even if your baby is making a lot of noise, it's honestly OK and we really don't want you to be uncomfortable about it.") Pay particular attention to what happens if a child makes enough noise to drown out the minister at any point. What is the body language of the adults sitting around you? Are they uptight and annoyed, or are they amused? Most tellingly, how does the preacher handle it? Does he soldier on without missing a beat, or does he acknowledge the sound, making a joke or comment designed to set the parents at ease?

See if the church has tried to make it easier for parents with small children to attend the worship service. Some congregations set aside a corner in which preschoolers can sit on the floor and color. I recently visited a church in Berkeley that had furnished an area near the front of the sanctuary with a rug, a basket of stuffed toys, and several rocking chairs for families with infants and toddlers.

When you bring your children with you on visits, notice how many adults, other than the parents of other young children, ask to be introduced to your children when they greet you. Truly kid-friendly churches are filled with people, including childless adults and the parents of grown children, who honestly delight in the presence of young children. They will want to be introduced to your kids because they can't wait to get to know them.

FINDING A CHURCH YOU AND YOUR KIDS WILL LIKE
Don't forget, as you are busily checking out what churches will offer your child, to pay attention to how well they will serve your needs. And if you're thinking that you'll ignore that advice because you intend to drop your kids off for Sunday school and head out for a tennis game, I urge you to reconsider. There must be something you want for your children that you believe they will find in church. Why else are you thinking about looking for one? If you have only a drive-by relationship to church, your kids might well be tempted to remain similarly removed.

Deciding What You Want for Your Children
For many of us, a deep-seated yearning that we are incapable of completely understanding, much less articulating, brings us to church. If that is the case for you, it is appropriate to rely on your intuitive responses when you choose a congregation to fulfill your longing. When you are deciding what you want for your children in a church home, gut-level responses will still play a big role. But you might want to layer in a level of reason-directed considerations on top of them.

In weighing the merits of big Sunday school programs versus small ones, you will want to consider your child's personality and social needs. Until she reached middle school age, my daughter was more oriented to adults than to her peers. Rosie never minded that the small Sunday school

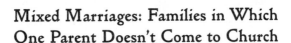

Mixed Marriages: Families in Which One Parent Doesn't Come to Church

I know a number of families in which one parent—usually a mother, although there are some exceptions—wants to go to church while her partner is ambivalent, conflicted, or indifferent. People in this situation need to realistically assess how likely it is that the reluctant parent might one day join a faith community. If you end up admitting that it's unlikely you will ever get your mate to come to church with you, charge on ahead, consulting only your and your child's preferences. On the other hand, if you think you've got a shot at having the whole family attend church together, you might want to sacrifice some of the things that are less important to you in favor of a congregation that will appeal more strongly to your partner.

Susan attended a liberal American Baptist church as a child. Brian, who had been raised in a fairly conservative Roman Catholic community, had rejected the religion and politics of his youth and embraced progressive and liberal ideals in all areas of his adult life. Neither of them had gone to church with any regularity since college, but they had a long-standing tacit agreement that they would raise their children with some religious instruction. Sue decided it was past time to find a church when her oldest child was in second grade. Her friends Mike and Elaine invited her to come with them to the Episcopal church they'd just joined, and she felt as if she'd found exactly what she was looking for: a congregation of kindred souls, a community service program that she could plug right into, and a Sunday school that already included her daughter's best friend. She brought the rest of the family with her the following Sunday, and the three kids were as enthusiastic as she was. Susan counted herself lucky that she'd found the perfect church home with such ease. After a few months, however, she noticed that Brian more often than not decided that he needed to catch up on his work on Sunday morning. At this point, Susan thought about what she really wanted for her family and what she needed to do to get it. "Brian was a little sheepish when I pressed him on it, but he finally confessed that even though he really liked St. Mark's, it didn't feel to him as if it counted, because it wasn't Catholic," Susan told me. "The area where we live has such a conservative bishop that I hadn't seriously considered looking at Catholic churches. But I knew that what I really wanted was for church to be an important part of our life as a family, and that wouldn't happen without Brian." So this wise woman quit the church that would have been the perfect choice for her alone and went looking for a Catholic church. She found a newly formed parish with a high percentage of families and a progressive young priest, where her entire family now worships together every Sunday.

Even if you are married to someone whose belief system makes it unlikely he or she will join you at church, you might want to consider your partner's sensibilities as you make your choice. Your agnostic mate might find it easier to have conversations with your children about what they learned in Sunday school if the vocabulary they are taught with is more along the lines of "Ten Best Ways to Live" than Ten Commandments, for instance. Some Sunday school curricula are more definitive than others about religious truths; it will be a lot easier on your Zen practitioner husband if your kids don't come home from Sunday school talking about "the one true way" and how everybody else is going to hell.

Finally, many families with the more traditional mixed-faith profile of Jewish and Christian have found the Unitarian Universalist Church, which draws equally on the two traditions,

continued from page 65

to be a good choice. (For more detail, see the sidebar on page 92.) Other families have chosen to join a faith community that matches the background of the more reluctant parent—especially when it is the minority tradition. My friend Ann, who went to Catholic school for almost as many years as I did, married a Jewish man whose family had never been observant. Even though Ann passionately believes in the value of religious education for children while Jeff is indifferent, Ann decided that their family should join a Jewish community. "If we joined a church, I know that Jeff would never come. Now, he at least comes to temple for high holy days," she says. "Also, American culture is so steeped in Christian symbolism that my kids will learn about that piece of their heritage willy-nilly . . . and my mother will fill in the holes the Christmas TV specials leave. Without the temple, there would be no one to teach them about their Jewishness." The Bay Area has a particularly large number of Jewish communities that welcome mixed-faith families and that are particularly accommodating to individuals of other beliefs.

program at our church rarely included a girl her own age, because she reveled in the attention lavished on her by the adults in the congregation. In some ways, I think she was even glad that there weren't too many kids her age around to compete for their affections. My son, however, is gregarious and peer-identified. If there isn't a boy his age in Sunday school, he is extremely unhappy—and makes sure that his parents know it. Fortunately for us, there happen to be a large number of families with boys Maguire's age at St. Aidan's right now. If there weren't, I'm afraid we would have to either go out and recruit a slew of Sunday school pals or look for a bigger church with a larger pool of little boys, because Maguire would be miserable with no companions.

Kids expect to discuss what they've learned in the vocabulary with which they've been taught, so it is important that the curriculum of the

Sunday school in the church you select is a comfortable fit with your own beliefs. It is conceivable, for instance, that you could find a church that warmly embraces spiritual seekers yet runs a very traditional Sunday school. While you are praying to the Mother/Father in the worship service, your children could be learning all about that old guy with the flowing white beard. When the chief reason you set out to find a church in the first place was your desire to see your child receive a religious education, it is a terrible irony to find yourself undermining that education because you quarrel with some of the tenets or cannot feel authentic using the language. At any church that you like well enough to seriously consider, you should ask the person in charge of Sunday school—who could be a Sunday school director or a Christian education director or a youth minister—to talk to you about the Sunday school curriculum and philosophy. Many congregations have some sort of written description of what they're trying to do in church school and may even be able to give you a sample of the curriculum they use.

Exploratory Visits

I recommend doing the first round of exploratory visits on an adults-only basis. The problems inherent in trying to collect impressions of a church with a fractious toddler or unpredictable infant in tow are obvious. What might not be so evident is that children who are old enough to sit quietly beside you during the whole service or to trot happily off to Sunday school are also old enough to have opinions and to form inconvenient ones. It's far wiser, if you ask me, to do the preliminary research on your own and bring the offspring to the second and third visits to churches you're seriously considering. You can thus avoid the ugly clash of wills that could well ensue after your nine-year-old discovers a long-lost preschool pal in the Sunday school class of the church whose pastor you instantly pegged as an old-fashioned sexist.

For many (if not most) of the coupled parents among my friends who have looked for churches in recent years, one partner in the relationship was the prime mover in the church-shopping endeavor. I recommend that this individual venture forth to do the exploratory visits solo and come home to share impressions and opinions with the parent who stayed home. The parents can then jointly come up with the short list of churches that merit additional visits by the whole family.

Single parents will probably find it easiest to just bring their babies or toddlers along on the exploratory church visits. School-age children, however, might be better off playing at a friend's house while you go on at least the first round of visits.

Bringing Your Children on a Church Visit

After you have narrowed your choices down to the short list of churches that are acceptable to you, it's time to let your children have a vote. You should have them attend the Sunday school or nursery program they would be enrolled in if you joined the church, so they can get a taste of what you are proposing they do on Sunday mornings. You too should attend some if not all of the Sunday school class. Even if your children are among the rare kids who cheerfully allow their parents to toddle off after plopping them into a room full of strangers, you will want to see the children's program in action yourself. This is your chance not only to assess the content and tone of the Sunday school teaching but also to observe the setting and the players so that you'll know what your kids are talking about when they tell you what they like or dislike.

If you bring your infant or toddler to the nursery program, you will probably need to stay for at least a while. Use the time to observe how the caregivers work with the other children and what they do to make your child more comfortable with them. Check to see if there is an adequate number of adults to care for the children. If they seem short-handed, ask the person in charge if it is a typical Sunday—you might be observing a fluke, a week in which a rush of visitors with babies appeared.

In many churches, school-age children join the congregation for part of the service. In some places, the kids sit with their parents for the beginning of the service and then troop off together; in others, the kids start off in Sunday school and come back for the end of the service; in still others, kids are present for both the start and the finish of the service. Sometimes children sit together, attended by their teacher, when they rejoin the service, and in other churches they sit with their families. If your children are off in Sunday school, either they will materialize by your side at some point (guided by some helpful adult) or you will notice them among a crowd of short heads near the front of the church. In either scenario, you don't have to do anything, so just relax. Most often, parents of the younger children in the nursery are responsible for retrieving them. In many churches, you can leave your infant or toddler in the nursery for the whole service, although you are generally welcome to come get him or her whenever you want. The policy should be clearly stated in the service bulletin or on a sign in the nursery room (or both).

Numerous programs for middle school and high school children are held at times that do not conflict with the main Sunday service, since youth, unlike children, are considered old enough to participate in the worship life of the congregation. Teenagers, in fact, are often encouraged to take part in a fairly rigorous education program leading up to confirmation, which becomes an important right of passage. You can arrange for your preteen or teenager to check out the appropriate youth group meeting, which might meet at an earlier time on Sunday morning or even during the week. As an adult, however, you might not be welcome to visit for as lengthy a period of time as you would be in Sunday school. The youth group leader or youth minister should be able to give you a good idea of what goes on, however, and many youth groups have regular parent information meetings.

How to Tell Whether a Church Is a Good Fit

In your final decision, the emotional response you and your children have to a given church will no doubt carry more weight than rational considerations, but it might be helpful (or at least reassuring) to review those reactions against a short checklist so that you can be sure you're being at least partly logical.

When you have found a church that feels right to you, ask yourself these questions:

1. If your child is the sort that needs buddies in order to be happy, are there enough kids of the appropriate age and gender in the church school program? As you consider this issue, keep in mind that many families do not come to church every Sunday. One or even two children of the right profile will probably not provide enough coverage for an intensely sociable kid.

2. How comfortable do you feel with the curriculum the church school uses? Practice talking to your kids about your own beliefs, using the vocabulary they hear in church school. Draw them out about what happened in Sunday school, and check your comfort level with what you hear them saying. Do you feel authentic? Can you imagine talking to your kids on a regular basis with these words? If anything they've learned makes you even a little uncomfortable, talk to someone—the education director, the Sunday school teacher, or the pastor—about it. You will be asking them not in order to request that they change anything but to make certain that you correctly understand what's going on. A particular lesson or phrase might give you the creeps because you think it means one thing, when in fact it was used to teach something else altogether.

3. Is it reasonable to expect that your family, given your current habits and preferences, will be able to arrive where they need to be when they need to be there most Sunday mornings? Most of us need to alter our Sunday morning routines somewhat to build the habit of church attendance into our lives. A family of night owls should probably think long and hard about joining a church all the way on the other side of town whose youth group meets at 9:00 a.m., even if that particular congregation was the universal favorite. No matter how much you love a given church, it won't mean much if you don't go two weeks out of four because you can't bear to get out of bed early enough. A number of congregations even offer family services in the early evening.

4. Are your kids willing to go to this particular church? Depending on their personalities and ages, it might be too much to ask to expect your children to actively want to go to the church you've chosen. They should at least be willing to go, however. Of course, if the objection is a generic one to Sunday school per se, that can be overcome in time. But if your child has developed a real antipathy to a particular church or Sunday school, you should seriously consider reopening your search.

Involving Children in the Final Decision

In the best of all possible worlds, your children will absolutely love the church that is shaping up as your prime favorite. Even if you allowed your children to visit only the congregations you thought would be acceptable to you, however, you might not be facing this ideal scenario. You could find yourself in a situation in which your children decide they absolutely love a church that has begun, upon more exposure, to leave you lukewarm at best. And of course your children could conceive a deep aversion to the parish that you have picked out as your ideal spiritual home. What to do?

You will want to figure out what is at the root of your differences before you go much further. Does your daughter see with innocent clear-sightedness something significant, either good or bad, that your muddy adult vision hasn't picked up? You might want to reevaluate. Or will it turn out that your son's decided preference for one church that isn't your top choice stems entirely from the outstanding doughnuts he was fed at coffee hour? Promise to stop by the bakery after church every Sunday. Truly serious objections from your children, of course, will probably cross a given church off your list, but most younger children will be easily persuaded, or bribed, to forget their minor preferences and go to Sunday school at whatever church you decide you want to join.

With children who are in middle school or older, however, you might want to give way to their preferences in the selection of a church, however lightweight or even silly the reasons might seem to you. It is in the preteen years, just as kids begin to look for fights to pick with their parents, that many church school programs become more open-ended. Many churches encourage middle schoolers to attend the main worship service. Classes or activities for this age group are held either before or after church or even on another day of the week. If your child is resistant to the church you've joined, a lack of enthusiasm could quickly sabotage your efforts to involve him or her in religious education.

ATTRIBUTES TO LOOK FOR IN A CHURCH

Part Three of this book includes contact information for a number of churches, along with lists of churches sorted by different attributes. These lists—which are constructed around hard data that is not to difficult to gather and is relatively easy to verify—are intended to function as clues for you to use in your search, rather than recommendations or judgments of individual churches. Nothing can substitute for your own investigation, but you might find it helpful to begin your search for a family church with churches that have one or more of these attributes:

Youth or Christian Education Minister

One concrete sign of a congregation's commitment to youth is having a staff member who is dedicated to young people; it is also likely that when that individual is an ordained member of the clergy, the church's financial commitment at least is pretty serious. This is not to say that all such churches truly love children or that churches without dedicated youth ministers don't. (In some cases, it probably has more to say about the size of the congregation or the depth of its pockets than anything else.) But you might want to take a look first at churches that offer such a good resource.

Junior Choir or Other Music Program for Children

Having a children's chorus or handbell choir can, again, be merely a sign that a given church is big enough to have a critical mass of children and the resources to hire a junior choir director. But it can also be a sign that a church values children enough to include them as full participants in worship, so it's worth checking out, particularly if your children are musical (or want to be).

Children Join the Congregation for the Entire Worship Service

One of the ways in which congregations live out their commitment to kids is through frequent intergenerational worship services, in which children and youth are invited to join as full participants in a liturgy that is designed to accommodate them as well as it does the adults. This practice is probably a bit easier for small churches than for big ones.

Big Sunday Schools

Congregations on this list will probably be of particular interest to families with children who want a large pool of potential friends in Sunday school. It also stands to reason that any church whose membership includes a high percentage of families with young children will tend to focus on them in ways that other congregations might not.

Regular Formal Programs for Teenagers

Some churches do not offer formal programs for teenagers, expecting that youth at this age will join the congregation at worship services and join in the regular activities of the community. Parents of preteens and teenagers who are looking for formal instruction or structured activities will want to look here first.

Finding an LGBT-Friendly Church

If you can bless boats and pets and retirements, you can
ask for God's blessings on significant relationships.

—PAM BYERS, EXECUTIVE DIRECTOR OF
COVENANT NETWORK OF PRESBYTERIANS

The good news about looking for a church that welcomes lesbians, gays, bisexuals, and transgendered (LGBT) individuals is that a lot of organizing around gay rights has already been done within churches. A host of organizations, position statements, and self-definitions already exist by which you will readily be able to recognize a congregation that embraces gays and lesbians as full members of their community. The bad news about looking for an LGBT-friendly church is that all that organizing was necessary in the first place: every mainline denomination includes conservatives who hold fast to the notion that homosexuality is some kind of sin. Happily, there is even more good news for those of us who live in the Bay Area: the Northern California regional authority of each mainline national church is in the forefront of support for gay rights. (Are we surprised?)

By way of background, some people believe that homosexuality is "inconsistent" with Scripture, with Christian faith, or with church doctrine. Conservatives most often point to two Old Testament passages to support their positions: Leviticus 18:22, "You shall not lie with a man as with a woman, it is an abomination," and Leviticus 20:13, "If a man lies with a male as with a woman, it is an abomination; they shall surely be put to death; their blood shall be upon them" (New Standard Revised Version).

The two issues through which churches are struggling to come to terms with homosexuality—primarily by way of legal proceedings at the national church level—are the ordination of openly gay clergy and the celebration of union ceremonies for same-sex couples.

CLUES FOR LGBT-FRIENDLY ATTITUDES

When Sarah and her lover, Joan, bought a house in Albany a few years ago, they became friendly with their next-door neighbor, a kindly older woman named Mary. One Saturday afternoon, during an over-the-back-fence chat, Mary invited Sarah to visit the local Presbyterian congregation with her, assuring her that she would like the church because it was *"reconciling,* you know." Well, Sarah didn't know, and she wasn't ready to go church shopping yet, so she put Mary off with a polite excuse and beat a hasty retreat into the house. Over the next few months, Mary renewed her invitation a few times, emphasizing each time that her church was a reconciling congregation. When Sarah finally decided to take Mary up on her invitation, she finally asked, "What are you talking about?" and so she learned what reconciling meant. "We welcome people like you!" Mary happily declared.

"Reconciling" is one of the words that can seem like part of a secret code to the uninitiated. In fact, there are a handful of words that churches use to declare their acceptance of sexual minorities. While there might be differences in the theology from which the terms flow, they all mean effectively the same thing. *Inclusive,* which means that the congregation makes a point of including everybody, refers to diversity of racial and economic background as well as of gender identity and sexual preference. "Inclusive" is therefore a more generic term that embraces rather than refers exclusively to acceptance of sexual minorities. *Reconciling* and *welcoming* mean the same thing—congregations who describe themselves thusly accept gays and lesbians completely. Episcopalians like the word "welcoming," while Presbyterians and Lutherans seem fond of "reconciling." The Methodists and UCC use *affirming* (most often in combination with "welcoming" or "open"), which has the added nuance of declaring, "Not only do we welcome LGBT folks to full membership in our church, we affirm to the world that their sexuality, like that of heterosexuals, is a gift of God." "Affirming" is used partially in response to the position of *confessing* congregations, who follow the "hate the sin but not the sinner" line of reasoning and say to LGBT people, "Sure, we will accept you, but we expect you to join us in praying that God will change your sinful sexual orientation."

Every one of the mainline denominations has a national group that advocates for LGBT rights, and several have local organizations as well. While some welcoming congregations might not have any formal designation as such, you might want to start your search by looking at the lists of churches in Part Three that are affiliated with the various church programs or organizations dedicated to LGBT rights. The other big clue to look for is whether or not a congregation celebrates same-sex unions; Part Three also includes a list of Bay Area churches that do.

CHURCH LAWS AND LGBT RIGHTS

When you learn about the official positions of the national church bodies, you may be tempted to forget about the whole church idea. All of the mainline denominations have been embroiled for several years now in passionate debates about homosexuality. To many of us in the Bay Area, it is incomprehensible that a discussion could actually be taking place in the twenty-first century, among seemingly intelligent and good-hearted people, about whether it is OK to be gay. To comprehend the dynamic without vilifying the participants, however, you need to realize that the national churches must accommodate the viewpoints of a hugely diverse body of folks from across the country—and they have not faced an issue this divisive in generations. There has been a lot of talk in the Presbyterian, United Methodist, and Episcopal national churches about the very real possibility of a schism, which means that the national church would break apart. Mostly everyone wants to avoid that. The national organizations are therefore coming up with responses designed to ward off a schism rather than to undertake fast-track change, regardless of how overdue it might be. (An overview of the current national church positions on gay rights can be found on page 80.) In any case, the reality of LGBT rights for most of the congregations in the Bay Area bears little resemblance to the policies made by the governing bodies of the national churches.

PREDOMINANTLY LGBT CHURCHES

There are churches that identify themselves as oriented primarily toward LGBT believers, and the makeup of their congregations reflects that emphasis. Some individual congregations in the mainline denominations fit this profile, usually as a result of the parish's location or the presence and special ministry of an openly gay or lesbian pastor.

The UNIVERSAL FELLOWSHIP OF METROPOLITAN COMMUNITY CHURCHES, or UFMCC (www.ufmcc.com), is is an entire mini-denomination primarily oriented toward LGBT communities. UFMCC was founded in 1968 in Los Angeles by a former Baptist minister, Troy Perry, and today has more than forty-two thousand members in over three hundred congregations. (See page 187 for a list of Bay Area MCC churches.)

CHURCHES THAT WELCOME LGBT FOLKS

Anyone who has no preference for one denomination or style of worship over another will soon ask an obvious question: Why should I bother doing all this decoding when there are churches that care primarily about people like me? Many people have no reason to look any further, and they find happy homes in churches with predominantly LGBT membership.

Others find that what they are looking for is something more easily found in a congregation that is welcoming to sexual minorities, rather than primarily oriented toward them. Jeffrey, a single gay man who moved to San Francisco from Southern California, looks to his church not only as his spiritual home but also as a base from which to build his social community. "I was looking for a well-rounded mix of people," he says. "My church has gay men, but it also has a lot of families with little kids, some older people, and people from many different ethnic backgrounds. I feel that making friends at church is one way that I can avoid ghettoizing my life." As Jeffrey points out, meeting other gay men is relatively easy for him at work in the financial industry and at the apartment complex where he lives in Diamond Heights. "There are plenty of ways for me to meet other gay men. For example, I just put a profile up on bear.net to find guys who are interested in friendship or maybe romance. But there's no place I can run a personal ad that says 'GWM seeks family to get to know and hang out with.' Well, I suppose I could place the ad, but who would answer it?"

Jim, a gay man in a committed relationship, chose the same congregation as Jeffrey did, for similar reasons. "I don't have any nieces or nephews of my own, and I really want to have children in my life. I see these kids, whose parents I know, in church week after week. I take my turn, along with everyone else, helping out in Sunday school once or twice a year. I have become the gay uncle to some of these kids I've known for a few years. They sit next to me at church functions, and we have something to talk about. I look forward to our encounters, and I think they do, too. I don't know where else I would be able to get to know children this gradually and naturally."

It might be a good idea to think about how you expect a faith community to fit into your life. Many people want to explore their spirituality in a focused way with other gays and lesbians, and an LGBT-identified church is probably the exact right answer for them. Folks who are interested in having their church community fill out their lives with the types of people they don't encounter at work or in their existing social network will want to consider a welcoming church whose membership is a mix of sexual identities and more traditional family configurations.

If you decide that what you're looking for is a more traditional church in one of the mainline denominations, your first task is to locate the congregations that welcome and affirm LGBT people. Part Three of this book contains a list of congregations in the Bay Area that have declared themselves in some formal and public way—generally by some sort of association with one or more of the LGBT rights groups in their denomination—as being completely accepting of sexual minority believers. In addition, there is a list of congregations whose pastors have indicated that they perform blessings for same-sex partners.

The following are some cross-denominational LGBT-identified online resources, many of which have lists of congregations that have officially declared themselves to be welcoming to lesbians and gays:

WHOSOEVER (www.whosoever.org) is an online magazine "intended for the spiritual growth of anyone who believes that God made gays, lesbians, bisexuals, and transgendered persons just the way they are, and is not asking them to change to be a part of God's kingdom." Whosoever has a list of welcoming congregations on its site.

ABOUT.COM has a great LGBT Directory of Faith Communities at www.gaylesissues.about.com/library/gfg/blgfg.htm.

GAY RIGHTS OVERVIEW BY DENOMINATION

In all of the mainline denominations, the same pattern holds true: The official church policies on gay rights issues are clearly in flux. Over the past twenty-five years, gay rights advocates have been pushing an ecclesiastical legislative agenda that would move the churches closer to official acceptance of the ordination of gay ministers and the blessing of same-sex unions. Conservatives have counterattacked with proposed legislation that would make the policies even less gay-friendly than they are now. In recent years, the heat of the struggle has increased, and most denominations are now engaged in a formal national dialogue about homosexuality and diversity. Meanwhile, the local governing authorities (with the exception of the American Baptists of the West) in the Bay Area are among the most liberal in the country and are in the forefront of advocacy within their national church for LGBT rights.

Presbyterian

SAME-SEX BLESSINGS: In May 2000, the Permanent Judicial Commission of the Presbyterian Church USA (PCUSA), the denomination's highest court, ruled that Presbyterian ministers may perform "holy union" ceremonies for gay and lesbian couples, as long as they don't call it marriage. A conservative legislative backlash has formed.

ORDINATION OF GAY CLERGY: PCUSA still bans the ordination of noncelibate homosexuals, but the Judicial Commission clarified recently that it is choosing not to extend the prohibition to seminarians and candidates for ministry.

LOCAL PRACTICE: The National Covenant Network of Presbyterians, the group that is pushing to get the national church to allow holy union ceremonies, comes out of the San Francisco Presbytery. It is widely believed that, should the national church decide to leave same-sex ceremonies up to the discretion of the local presbyteries, San Francisco would immediately embrace them.

DENOMINATION-SPECIFIC LGBT RIGHTS ORGANIZATIONS:
More Light Presbyterians (www.mlp.org).
Presbyterian Parents of Gays and Lesbians, Inc.
(www.presbyterianparents.org).
Covenant Network of Presbyterians (www.covenantnetwork.org). Formed in 1997 to work on getting the standards of ordination amended to be friendlier to gays and lesbians.
That All May Freely Serve (www.tamfs.org). Works for the ordination of LGBT individuals.

Episcopal

The Episcopal Church USA (ECUSA) is in a state similar to that of PCUSA: Over the past several years, people who support LGBT rights have been pushing the church dialogue on human sexuality by introducing resolutions that would allow the blessing of same-sex unions and the ordination of openly gay clergy. Conservative Episcopalians are horrified at what they perceive as the drift of the church in a profoundly wrong direction and have taken up active resistance. A network of approximately twenty conservative congregations has broken with the Episcopal Church over its stand on human sexuality.

SAME-SEX BLESSINGS: The official act that put conservatives over the edge was the passage, by a substantial margin, of a resolution at the 2000 General Convention (the annual national meeting of the church body) stating that the church should offer "pastoral support" to couples in relationships outside of marriage. A resolution that called for rites to "support relationships of mutuality and fidelity other than marriage" was defeated, however.

ORDINATION OF GAY CLERGY: Although many conservative leaders in the Episcopal Church decry the ordination of gays, there is currently no ecclesiastical legislative push to formalize acceptance of the practice, since it is openly done in many places and bishops who ordain gays and lesbians are not prosecuted by the national church authorities.

LOCAL PRACTICE: The Bishop of California, whose diocese includes the Bay Area, declared in an address to his peers from across the country, "I've ordained more gays and lesbians than anyone in history." Many Bay Area Episcopal priests perform blessings on same-sex unions.

DENOMINATION-SPECIFIC LGBT RIGHTS ORGANIZATIONS:
Alliance of Lesbian and Gay Anglicans (www.alga.org).

Integrity (www.integrityusa.org). Their web site is a good source of up-to-date information on the progress of gay rights initiatives throughout the Episcopal Church USA.

Oasis, California (www.oasiscalifornia.org). The gay and lesbian ministry of the Diocese of California (roughly San Francisco, Marin, Alameda, Contra Costa, and San Mateo Counties). The web site has a list of churches that support Oasis in various ways and that have made the public commitment to be welcoming.

Beyond Inclusion (www.beyondinclusion.org).

Methodist

The issue of homosexuality has been at the center of torturous debate in the United Methodist Church (UMC) since 1972. Things came to a head at the national church's General Conference in 2000, at which delegates voted, by substantial margins, to reaffirm the church's position on homosexuality as "incompatible with Christian teaching" and to retain other restrictive bans, including a prohibition against using official church funds for any organization or program that promotes homosexuality as an acceptable lifestyle. Hundreds of Methodists protested the results of these votes, and thirty people, including two bishops, were removed from the conference floor and arrested, in an unprecedented intervention by local police.

SAME-SEX BLESSINGS: This is the front on which church members are currently working through the issue of the UMC's position toward gays and lesbians. Although the denomination officially prohibits same-sex blessings, activists have been using the tactic of conducting high-profile ceremonies that bless same-sex relationships as a means of pushing for change. In the past, clergy have been defrocked and otherwise disciplined for doing so; given the climate in the national organization, such punishments are likely to continue.

ORDINATION OF GAY CLERGY: While there has long been a ban on the ordination of openly gay individuals, numerous gays and lesbians have been ordained as UMC ministers. The wiggle room comes from the degree to which a candidate for ordination announces his or her sexual orientation to church authorities.

LOCAL PRACTICE: The Western Jurisdictional Conference (covering ten Western states) has approved, almost unanimously, a statement entitled "We Will Not Be Silent," in which they basically say that they can't accept discrimination against LGBT folks.

DENOMINATION-SPECIFIC LGBT RIGHTS ORGANIZATIONS:
Reconciling Ministries Network (www.rcp.org). Their web site has a list of reconciling congregations and campus ministries.

Affirm: United Methodists for Lesbian, Gay, Bisexual, and Transgendered Concerns (www.umaffirm.org).

Methodist Federation for Social Action (www.olg.com/mfsa/). While not exclusively oriented to sexual minority rights, MFSA has been a key player in the coalition of groups that is working on LGBT rights within the UMC.

Lutheran

The Evangelical Lutheran Church in America (ELCA) is now officially in a period of highly structured discussion about the place of gays and lesbians in the life of the church. Church leaders are clearly hoping that with a thorough and systematic discernment process they can avoid the bitter disagreements that are rocking other denominations.

SAME-SEX BLESSINGS: ELCA bishops have advised pastors that they do not approve of ceremonies blessing same-sex relationships, though two ELCA synods (Greater Milwaukee and Southeast Michigan) have adopted resolutions that open the door for their pastors to perform them. Thus far no ECLA pastors have been prosecuted for performing same-sex blessings.

ORDINATION OF GAY CLERGY: The ELCA standards for ordination clearly state that practicing homosexuals are ineligible for ordained ministry in the church. The key word is "practicing," because church policy further spells out that the problem is not whether you are "homosexual in your self-understanding" but whether you are engaged in a sexual relationship with someone of your own gender.

Ordination standards, rather than same-sex ceremonies, have been the hot-button issue for the ELCA thus far. The national church maintains an official roster of clergy who are eligible to be hired as pastors by ELCA congregations. Openly gay individuals have been taken off this roster, and churches that hire a pastor not on the roster run the risk of being disciplined, which could even involve being expelled from the denomination.

LOCAL PRACTICE: When the University Lutheran Chapel in Berkeley hired as its pastor a gay activist who was not on the roster of approved clergy, it was censured by the local bishop. He made it very clear, however, that although he personally disagrees with the national church's policy on the ordination of gay clergy, he felt he had to respond to an act of ecclesiastical disobedience that could have negative implications for the whole denomination. The rest of the congregations in the Sierra Pacific synod rallied around University Lutheran Chapel, and the bishop ultimately declined to take disciplinary action against the chapel and invited it to be a resource in the synod's ongoing discussion of LGBT issues.

DENOMINATION-SPECIFIC LGBT RIGHTS ORGANIZATIONS:

Lutherans Concerned North America (www.lcna.org). Their web site includes a list of the more than a hundred congregations that have signed on to the Reconciling in Christ program, through which churches identify themselves as welcoming to gays and lesbians.

Lutheran Lesbian and Gay Ministries (www.llgm.org).

Network for Inclusive Vision (PO Box 16313, San Diego, CA 92176).

The Extraordinary Candidacy Project (www.extraordinarycandidacy project.org). Works to promote the full participation of sexual minorities in the professional ministry of the Lutheran Church.

Baptist

American Baptist Churches USA (ABC), the most liberal of the Baptist branches, passed a resolution via the General Board in 1992 stating that "the practice of homosexuality is incompatible with Scripture." Some of the local authorities, including those in th Bay Area, have followed that up with anti-gay resolutions. The flash point for American Baptists is congregations that proclaim their welcoming stance by becoming members of the Association of Welcoming and Affirming Baptists, or AWAB (users.aol.com/wa baptists/). In 1996 the ABC West region "disfellowshipped" or expelled four congregations that refused to relinquish their association with AWAB. Meanwhile, although the denomination might seem inhospitable to LGBT folks, the disfellowshipped congregations (which have thus far been able to maintain an association with the national church) are among the most gay-friendly churches around, including one (First Baptist in Berkeley) whose pastor is openly lesbian and as well as an ecumenical gay rights activist.

Other Denominations

The 204 regional associations of the UNITED CHURCH OF CHRIST (UCC) set their own policies, and several have ordained openly gay or lesbian people. The church's national body of delegates, the General Synod, has urged the associations not to deny ordination solely because of a candidate's sexual orientation. The United Church of Christ Coalition for Lesbian, Gay, Bisexual, and Transgender Concerns (www.coalition.simplenet.com) is the officially recognized advocacy group to the national church. Their Open and Affirming program (ONA) identifies UCC congregations that declare themselves as LGBT-friendly—their web site even numbers the four hundred or so congregations in the order in which they signed up for the program, so that you can see who was serious enough to sign up early!

As in so many other matters, the official policies of the UNITARIAN UNIVERSALIST ASSOCIATION (UUA) are among the most humane and progressive you will find. Unitarians have been on record as supporting the rights of gay people since 1970. They support openly gay and lesbian ministers and Ceremonies of Union for same-sex couples. They've had an Office of Bisexual, Gay, Lesbian, and Transgender Concerns since 1973 and have a hugely successful welcoming congregations program. Interweave is an LGBT-identified membership organization associated with the UUA.

ATTRIBUTES TO LOOK FOR IN A CHURCH

Part Three of this book includes contact information for a number of churches, along with lists of churches sorted by different attributes. These lists—which are constructed around hard data that is not to difficult to gather and is relatively easy to verify—are intended to function as clues for you to use in your search, rather than recommendations or judgments of individual churches. See page 187 for church listings for the LGBT-oriented Metropolitan Community Churches, and the gay-friendly Unitarian Universalists.

Nothing can substitute for your own investigation, but you might find it helpful to begin your search for a church within a mainline denomination among that churches that appear on these lists:

Affiliated with an LGBT Advocacy Group

The churches on this list have made a formal affiliation with an advocacy group, either an ecumencial one or one that is specific to their denomination, or have officially signed on to be designated as welcoming, affirming, or reconciling—all of which mean gay-friendly.

Parish Mission Statement Includes the Words "Inclusive" or "Welcoming"

This is a little arbitrary, since many congregations' mission statements use different words that convey essentially the same spirit. Most often, a congregation that has chosen one of these words to include in its mission statement has done so to deliberately encompass LGBT folks. So you should take inclusion on this list as a definite sign that a particular church is gay-friendly, but you should in no way interpret omission from the list to indicate that another church is not.

Same-Sex Blessings

Even taking into account that the stakes are much higher in certain denominations than in others for clergy who choose to act in defiance of their national church's official position, I would say this is pretty bottom line. Again, don't assume that a church not on this list is against them.

Finding a Church for Spiritual Seekers, Cultural Creatives, and Political Progressives

He died to take away your sins, not your mind.

—SLOGAN FROM AN EPISCOPAL CHURCH ADVERTISING CAMPAIGN

Despite the fact that I grew up in a staunchly church-going family and married the son of an Episcopalian priest, joining a church was one of the more radical acts of my adult life. I knew that I wanted my daughter to go to Sunday school, but it took me a long time to recognize my own craving for a church life because it was so inconsistent with my definition of myself. I had always thought that if I were going to have a spiritual practice (which I did intend to get to someday, honest), it was probably going to be Zen. The aesthetics of Zen practice are impeccable, its political associations in latter-day America are irreproachable, and it's cool to boot—look at all those Beat poets who took it up.

Probably because I knew too many working-class Catholic Democrats, I never made the error of equating Christianity with the Christian Right. But I nevertheless entered the experience of church-going with a stand-offish attitude. I intended to do it undercover; I would mumble the words, enjoy belting out the hymns, and then slide stealthily out the door. I assumed that everybody else at the church would be there because they believed, literally, in everything I'd been taught as a child. The last thing I expected was that a Christian church, and a mainline denomination at that, would either welcome or serve the real me. I was much more certain about what I didn't believe than I was about what I did. I hadn't been to church as anything other than a polite visitor at Christmas services for nearly twenty years, but I still harbored some lingering resentment from those long-ago days when I was rousted from bed every Sunday morning and made to scramble into my dress-up clothes and then sit through an interminable and boring Mass with perfectly dreadful music.

Ironically, of all the people I had in mind when I set out to write this book, the category I belong to—assorted unconventional types whose friends will surely give them a hard time about going to church—is the most difficult to address. Churches don't have formal ministries to unbe-lievers, as they do for children and families. Neither do denominations dis-criminate against them in the way they do against sexual minorities, so there are no organized rights groups for us heathens. And, frankly, many churches don't give a damn about our aesthetic and political sensitivities.

So I'm going to attempt to help you find a faith community by describ-ing the attributes common to churches that are comfortable for us uncon-ventional types. You could then begin your search by looking in the directory in Part Three of this book to find churches that have many of these attributes. Actually, allow me back up for a moment and suggest that you might want to consider two religious traditions that are in some ways the Western equivalents of Zen in the cool department, the Unitarian Universalist Association (see page 92), and the Religious Society of Friends (see page 97). Read on if you've decided against that route and are looking for a compatible mainline congregation.

CHURCHES THAT APPEAL TO UNCONVENTIONAL TYPES

Needless to say, what follows is neither prescriptive nor infallible. The most conservative pastor you encounter might be a woman, there are churches chock-full of creative nonconformists that have absolutely traditional liturgies, and you might find a congregation that uses inclusive language yet insists on a certain set of beliefs. Nevertheless, I suggest that you look first at churches that have most of the characteristics on the list that follows.

Uses Inclusive Language in Worship Services

Most progressive-minded churches rewrite their denomination's prayer book and use translations of the Bible that avoid overtly assigning a gender to God. That can mean using "she" in reference to the deity, rewording sentences to avoid the use of personal pronouns, and including references to the "Mother/Father," among other things. This inclusive language of justice and equality can also take on the imagery of God and the ways in which you evoke the people's relationship to the Supreme Being. Anything that calls up the all-too-familiar God the Father is generally avoided; you will hear a variety of addresses, including "Creator," "Abba," and "Spirit."

Traditional translations of the Bible, such as the King James Version, and many of the denominational prayer books, are beautifully crafted texts, while inclusive-language versions are more consistently inoffensive than sublime. Thus, not all critics of inclusive language—of which there are plenty—object to the intention behind it so much as to the aesthetics of the execution.

Has Female and/or Openly Gay Clergy

Obviously, many forward-thinking congregations have heterosexual male pastors. Given the presence in every mainline denomination of conservative elements, this attribute is simply a handy sorting tool. Most congregations choose their lead clergy, so it's a pretty safe bet that a congregation with a female or openly gay pastor is unlikely to be hidebound and traditional in its thinking. You won't want to cross a church off your list simply because it has a straight man at the helm, but you will probably want to add churches with female or gay clergy to it.

Unitarians Can Be a Little Smug Sometimes
(Of Course, They Have Every Reason to Be . . .)

I had a friend in college, Cathleen Schreiner, who was the most positive-thinking individual I've ever met. She was full of energy, she was efficient, she had goals. She had no tolerance for negativity. Whenever I would voice criticism or doubt about any of our mutual acquaintances (and I'm sorry to have to tell you that my attitude in those days had much more "oh no" in it than "can do"), Cathleen would instantly comment, "Oh, you're just jealous." That response was so automatic that I found it easy to dismiss until the day I felt the nasty little lurch in my stomach that told me this time she was right: I was jealous of the transfer student who'd just landed on our dorm floor after her semester abroad—the woman who was really funny and really smart and looked so French in her fashion-forward thrift-store dresses. True, she might not have had the best judgment about men, but who cared?

I feel the same painful tug every time I voice the clever little observation "Unitarians can be a little smug sometimes." A number of the Unitarians I know are a little smug, just as the big-city parents I know who send their kids to public school are. But who cares? They have reason to be, and I only notice because I'm jealous. Living in the hostile-to-organized-religion, lefty intelligentsia, vaguely artsy-fartsy milieu I do, it gives me a pang to have to admit it, faithful Episcopalian that I am, but the Unitarian Universalist Association is about the coolest denomination around.

Liberal is built right into Unitarians' definition of themselves. Even if that didn't deter some conservatives from slipping in, they wouldn't have any ground on which to do any Bible-thumping, because Unitarianism is a non-creedal religion. Unitarians believe that personal experience, conscience, and reason should be the final authorities in religion. And while they might not label themselves as such, these folks are anarchists: Authority is decentralized and resides in each individual, self-governing congregation. Unitarianism draws equally from the Christian and Jewish traditions, and social justice is its middle name.

So here I am: I joined a church that's part of a mainline denomination. In fact, some of the reasons I was drawn to my dear little church stem from its connection to the Anglican tradition. Our denomination, in so many ways gracious and open-minded, is still in the throes of a debate over whether it's wrong to be homosexual. Even though they have been ordaining women as priests since 1974, there are still three bishops who won't ordain women and won't hire them, either. I find myself in the position of having to defend (and I do feel defensive) my association with this organization to my friends, many of whom are predisposed to think organized religion is evil in any case.

My Unitarian acquaintances, on the other hand, can calmly point to the fact that their General Assembly passed resolutions in 1970 saying, essentially, "We affirm that women and sexual minorities have full rights in our world; we are going to work for their rights in the greater world, and we urge all of our congregations to do everything they can to promote and support women and LGBT folks into positions of leadership, including ordained ministry." In 1984, the General Assembly passed a business resolution that said, in effect, "We're still on record as affirming the full equality of sexual minority individuals, and by the way the only reason we don't do same-sex marriages is that they're illegal. So we are going on record here as saying that the services of union many of our ministers are performing for same-sex couples are a terrific idea, and let's do everything we can to support them—for instance, let's print up some materials to give people ideas on how to do these rites and circulate them around."

continued from page 93

Many people think the Unitarian Universalist Association is the obvious (some would say only) choice for freethinking progressive types. I feel like the mother of an awkward, homely boy who doesn't have many friends and isn't doing very well in school. My love for my child is no less fierce because I feel more than a bit green when my neighbor tells me that her son, the class president who's been high scorer two basketball seasons in a row, made National Merit Finalist. It's entirely possible that she's not smug and that I'm just defensive. Maybe it's a little bit of both.

Check it out: www.uua.org has links to a number of local web sites. See page 187 for a complete list of the Unitarian congregations in San Francisco, Marin, Alameda, San Mateo, and Santa Clara Counties.

Celebrates Some Sort of Same-Sex Blessing Ceremony

Like the previous attribute, this is mostly a gross sorting tool to locate churches you might want to look at, rather than ones you want to eliminate from consideration. Some of the most forward-thinking congregations around might not be able to perform same-sex blessings because of the current political climate in their national church.

Has Members from a Mixture of Religious Backgrounds

The previous rector of my church would laugh when he told the story of looking out over the congregation when the service reached the creed, the litany of things you say you believe. He described it as watching a wave moving around the room. The volume would rise and fall as pockets of people fell silent when the prayer book's creed made a declaration they didn't concur with. In some places, his was the only audible voice. There was a continual mumble trailing behind, as half the people changed all the "he's" to "she's," the "Lords" to "Gods," and the "Fathers" to "Mother/Fathers." Eventually, it started to drive him nuts, so he began to eliminate the creed from the service.

When I heard that story, I thought to myself, "That's what I love about this place." Although many of the congregation are deeply spiritual, even pious in the conventionally churchy sense, I think we all agree that the journey is more important than the destination, the answer is less important than the work of authentically grappling with the question. It is more a community of seekers than a community of believers. If you've been holding back from going to church because you're afraid of finding yourself alone amidst a group of people who all know what they firmly believe, while you have a collection of doubts and questions, you'll want to join up with some seekers, too.

When I tried to figure out how to isolate this characteristic into a piece of data that people who are church shopping could be on the lookout for, I thought about the fact that "cradle Epsicopalians" who grew up in the church are actually in the minority at St. Aidan's. This makes sense. People who have more questions than answers often look farther afield than the tradition they grew up with. Many individuals who feel disaffected with or even wounded by the religion of their youth struggle as adults with what they believe. Congregations with a high percentage of people who are still worshipping in the only denomination they've ever known have less of a seeker's orientation. If you are wrestling with what you believe, people who settled those questions a long time ago are probably not the best company for you. On the other hand, with a bunch of folks from two or three mainline Protestant flavors, mixed up with some fallen-away Catholics, a few jack Mormons, and a bunch of recovering agnostics, you're good to go.

Likes to Play with Liturgy

Certain churches pride themselves on what is known as "creative liturgy." Rather than using the denomination's prayer book or hymnal exclusively, they borrow services from their sister churches throughout the world, adapt rituals from other traditions, or simply write their own. Creative liturgies often involve nontraditional elements (like dance), unusual instrumentation (like guitars), and audience participation. If attending a worship service in a cathedral with a hundred-voice choir and professional soloists has a bit of the feel of attending a symphony performance, going to a church that involves the congregation in creative liturgy feels much more like community theater.

Since a certain amount of irreverence generally accompanies a willingness to play with the worship service, most congregations that do a significant amount of creative liturgy are progressively oriented and especially compatible to spiritual seekers. However, some of the most progressive and open-minded churches in the Bay Area don't do much at all in the way of creative liturgy. Certain considerations—many of them positive attributes of the more liturgically traditional congregations—make a church less likely to play with the worship service. It's easier to be a little out there when your congregation is small—for one thing, the people doing wacky stuff have a smaller audience, and for another, in a smaller community both satisfactions and dissatisfactions with new things make themselves known more easily. Larger churches, especially congregations that are diverse in terms of age as well as race and ethnicity, can be open and irreverent; it is simply more difficult for them to express those qualities through creative liturgy.

Uses Nontraditional Instrumentation

Although it may seem like a throwback to the seventies, guitar masses are alive and well, as are other kinds of church instruments besides an organ—pianos, drums, and marimbas, for instance. Churches that use only or primarily an organ for accompaniment are most likely to use traditional hymns and church music, most of which was composed with the organ in mind. Congregations that use other instruments tend to draw from a variety of music sources, including ecumenical ones—this often bespeaks a certain open-mindedness. In addition, when a variety of instruments are used it generally means that amateur musicians from the congregation are involved, while an organ is generally the sole province of the professional music director. This can be a sign of the "worship belongs to all of us" attitude that is often a sign of openness to lay leadership.

Offers Alternative Services

Many church-going people who were raised to go to church on Sunday morning and continued the practice into their adult lives find that the experience of the main Sunday morning worship is enough. Folks who are either returning to worship after a long absence or attending church for the first time in their lives, however, often find that they are looking for something either in addition to or in place of the main Sunday liturgy.

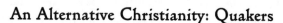

An Alternative Christianity: Quakers

The Religious Society of Friends, whose members are more commonly known as Quakers, emphasizes the personal experience of God in one's life. Their most distinctive beliefs are in the ministry of all believers, which means that they do without clergy, and in the importance of waiting silently to hear the inner voice that is God speaking to them in their hearts. Although a devotion to peace and service is universal among its members, Quakerism, as a non-creedal religion, embraces a diversity of beliefs, and many Friends nowadays deemphasize the Christian identity of their religion.

Friends in the "unprogrammed" tradition base their worship on expectant waiting. They gather in a plain room, facing each other, with no prearranged program of prayers or music. Everyone sits silently, trying to listen to the Spirit, until someone is moved to speak. That person stands, says what he or she has to say, and then sits down. Meetings generally last an hour, and it is not out of the ordinary for the whole hour to pass in silence.

In the unprogrammed tradition, congregations are known as monthly meetings, although they hold worship services weekly ("meeting" refers to something else). Some monthly meetings also have smaller assemblies, known as worship groups, under their wings. The web site www.quaker.org offers a short primer on Quaker beliefs as well as some lengthier articles on Quaker history and practices.

See page 187 for a listing of Quaker meetings in the Bay Area.

Alternative services, especially contemplative ones, are often the hallmark of a church with a high number of spiritual seekers. Some of these services have been a part of the Church for centuries; others are slightly New Agey contemporary inventions. The more common ones include the following:

TAIZÉ is an ecumenical Christian monastery in France that was founded in 1949. The brothers, inspired by the great monastic tradition, have created a liturgy of meditative common prayer with chants that were composed specifically to be easy to learn and sing. People from all over the world have traveled to Taizé to learn the liturgy, so many of the chants use short Latin phrases. Most churches that offer Taizé services do so on a weekday evening.

CONTEMPLATIVE PRAYER is Christian meditation. In the 1970s, three Trappist monks took the practices of the contemplative prayer tradition, which stretched back for many centuries, and distilled them into the *centering prayer* method, which is now used by people in different denominations. Meditative services that don't specifically use the centering prayer method are also sometimes called *quiet prayer* services.

HEALING PRAYER services are quieter, more intense, and often less structured than a big Sunday morning worship service. Healing ministers, both lay and ordained, do laying on of hands, and the congregation prays for those members of the community who have requested healing prayer.

COMPLINE and VESPERS are traditional evening services that have a quiet and reflective tone.

Values Lay Leadership

People who think for themselves tend to be happy to challenge authority when the occasion warrants. If you realize that an authoritarian pastor is unlikely to be a good match for you, you'll want to look for a church in which lay people—regular members of the congregation—are in leadership roles. When you visit a church, your antennae should go up if it seems as though nobody but the pastor can give you any information. Does the minister make all the announcements, or do other people report events in a tone of clear ownership? Look in the newsletter and see if you can sense whether or not other people besides the pastor are doing things like leading classes, forming small groups, and even preaching.

Works for Peace and Justice

Practically every church is involved in good works in some way or another, but in churches that are interested in progressive social causes you will encounter the words "peace" and "justice" a lot. You can look for these words in several places. Most churches have printed brochures, and many have web sites. This type of material includes both the description the church has written of itself and the list of organizations it is affiliated with. The church's weekly bulletin, which you are given at the worship service, and its newsletter will include notices about both the congregation's committees and the organizations that church members work with. Of course, any progressive community worth its salt will have some sort of environmental committee or program.

Most churches also have some sort of outreach program, through which they give away a certain percentage of the money they raise every year through pledges and fundraising. Lists of the gifts they've given are readily available, and you can see the types of groups the church has funded. Another good indicator of a church's social conscience is the percentage of its annual budget the congregation devotes to outreach. Activist congregations tend to tithe, or give away, at least 10 percent.

Thinks That There Is More Than One Way to the Truth

The Center for Progressive Christianity has come up with an eight-point definition of progressive Christianity that most (if not all) progressive churches subscribe to, even if they haven't formally affiliated with the center. You can view the whole list on their web site at www.tcpc.org. The second of these points reads "By calling ourselves progressive, we mean that we are Christians who recognize the faithfulness of other people who have other names for the gateway to God's realm." In other words, this way works for us, but it's not the only way. One of the ways a church that thinks this way declares itself is to have open Communion, by which anyone (sometimes anyone who is baptized) is invited to share in the Eucharist. Another way is to show evidence of interest in other traditions, such as interfaith services and education about other religions.

ATTRIBUTES TO LOOK FOR IN A CHURCH

Part 3 of this book includes contact information for a number of churches, along with lists of churches sorted by different attributes. These are intended to function as clues for you to use in your search, rather than recommendations or judgments of individual churches. Local Unitarian Universalist congregations, Metropolitan Community Churches, and Quaker meetings are listed on page 187.

Some of the qualities I've discussed above don't appear on any lists in Part Three—usually because I couldn't find a sufficiently reliable way of capturing the data through a questionnaire. You will need to sniff those attributes out as you visit churches. The following lists in Part Three might prove helpful, however, in drawing up a list of churches to start with.

- *Pastor Called by His or Her First Name*
- *Inclusive Language Is a Top Priority*
- *Female Lead Clergy*
- *Innovative or Creative Liturgical Style*
- *Nontraditional Instrumentation Used in Worship Services*
- *Nontraditional Texts Used in Worship Services*
- *Liturgical Dance Used in Worship Services*
- *Original Music or Liturgical Texts Created by Music Staff or Members of the Congregation*
- *Other Creative or Unusual Elements Used Regularly in Worship Services*
- *Affiliated with Center for Progressive Christianity*
- *Unofficial Dress Code Is "Play Clothes" Casual*
- *Same-Sex Blessings*
- *Parish Mission Statement Includes the Words "Inclusive" or "Welcoming"*
- *Alternative Services*

PART THREE

Data on Bay Area churches:
Lists of churches that share specific
attributes of interest to church shoppers,
listings of alternative churches, and
contact information for 400-plus
individual congregations

Lists of Churches with Certain Attributes

Each of the lists below groups together churches that have a particular quality or practice in common. These attributes can be useful as a preliminary selection tool when you are putting together a list of churches you think are worth a visit. The Church Listings section, which follows these lists of churches sorted by attributes, provides contact information for all the congregations included.

I compiled these lists from a questionnaire I developed and sent out to 400+ congregations in the Bay Area. Almost half of the churches filled out and returned the form, and it is those churches that appear on these lists. You should therefore look at these rosters as confirmation that a particular church does things a certain way, rather than as an indication that a church not on the list doesn't.

There are four categories of lists. The first consists of general attributes that anybody might find interesting. Each of the remaining three categories covers attributes of interest to one of the three groups this book addresses in depth: families with young children, lesbian/gay/bisexual/transgendered (LGBT) folks, and cultural creatives/political progressives.

If a given attribute is of particular interest to more than one group— same-sex blessings—for instance-that list appears in both sections. Even if you fall into one of the three special interest groups I've covered in depth, I really encourage you to scan all the attributes to select the ones you will pay the most attention to. After all, who knows better than you what you like?

ATTRIBUTES OF GENERAL INTEREST

- *Handbells*
- *Healing*
- *Incense*
- *Small Groups for Singles and/or Young Adults*

HANDBELLS
Churches that use handbells on a regular basis in their worship.

All Saints' Episcopal Church, Episcopal, San Francisco

Asbury UMC, United Methodist Church, Livermore

Bethany UMC, United Methodist Church, San Francisco

Christ Episcopal Church, Episcopal, Los Altos

Christ the Victor Lutheran Church, Lutheran, Fairfax

Church of the Advent of Christ the King, Episcopal, San Francisco

Community Church of Mill Valley, United Church of Christ, Mill Valley

Congregational Church of Belmont, United Church of Christ, Belmont

Covenant Presbyterian Church, Presbyterian, Palo Alto

Covenant Presbyterian Church, Presbyterian, San Francisco

Episcopal Church of St. Mary the Virgin, Episcopal, San Francisco

First Christian Church, Disciples of Christ, Palo Alto

First Congregational UCC, United Church of Christ, Alameda

First Congregational UCC, United Church of Christ, San Jose

First Presbyterian Church, Presbyterian, Newark

First Presbyterian Church, Presbyterian, Oakland

First Presbyterian Church, Presbyterian, San Leandro

First Presbyterian Church of Mountain View, Presbyterian, Mountain View

First UMC, United Methodist Church, Campbell

Grace Lutheran Church, Lutheran, Palo Alto

Hillsdale United Methodist, United Methodist Church, San Mateo

Hope Lutheran Church, Lutheran, Santa Clara

Lake Merritt UMC, United Methodist Church, Oakland

Los Gatos UMC, United Methodist Church, Los Gatos

New Creation Lutheran Church, Lutheran, San Jose

Presbyterian Church of Los Gatos, Presbyterian, Los Gatos

Presbyterian Church of Sunnyvale, Presbyterian, Sunnyvale

Redwoods Presbyterian Church, Presbyterian, Larkspur

St. Andrew Presbyterian Church, Presbyterian, Pacifica

St. Andrew's Episcopal Church, Episcopal, Saratoga

St. Edmund's Episcopal Church, Episcopal, Pacifica

St. Elizabeth's Episcopal Church, Episcopal, South San Francisco

St. Francis' Episcopal Church, Episcopal, San Francisco

St. Francis' Episcopal Church, Episcopal, San Jose

St. John-the-Evangelist Episcopal Church, Episcopal, San Francisco

St. Luke's Episcopal Church, Episcopal, Los Gatos

St. Mark's Episcopal Church, Episcopal, Palo Alto

St. Paul Lutheran Church, Lutheran, Oakland

St. Stephen's Episcopal Church, Episcopal, Belvedere

St. Stephens In-the-Field Episcopal Church, Episcopal, San Jose

Seventh Avenue Presbyterian Church, Presbyterian, San Francisco

Trinity Lutheran Church, Lutheran, Alameda

Trinity Presbyterian Church, Presbyterian, San Jose

Valley Presbyterian Church, Presbyterian, Portola Valley

West Valley Presbyterian Church, Presbyterian, Cupertino

HEALING

Churches that offer laying on of hands or healing at their main Sunday service and/or have a regular healing service.

All Saints' Episcopal Church, Episcopal, San Francisco

Christ Episcopal Church, Episcopal, Los Altos

Christ the King Lutheran Church, Lutheran, Fremont

Church of the Advent of Christ the King, Episcopal, San Francisco

Church of the Holy Innocents, Episcopal, Corte Madera

Congregational Church of Belmont, United Church of Christ, Belmont

Episcopal Church of the Incarnation, Episcopal, San Francisco

Episcopal Church of St. Mary the Virgin, Episcopal, San Francisco

Fairfax Community Church, United Church of Christ, Fairfax

First Christian Church, Disciples of Christ, San Mateo

First Congregational Church, United Church of Christ, Berkeley

First UMC, United Methodist Church, San Rafael

Good Shepherd Episcopal Church, Episcopal, Belmont

Grace Lutheran Church, Lutheran, Palo Alto

Holy Cross Episcopal Church, Episcopal, Castro Valley

Holy Innocents' Episcopal Church, Episcopal, San Francisco

Immanuel Lutheran Church, Lutheran, San Jose

Lutheran Church of Our Savior, Lutheran, San Francisco

Marin Lutheran Church, Lutheran, Corte Madera

New Life Church, Baptist, Richmond

Peace Lutheran Church, Lutheran, San Bruno

St. Aidan's Episcopal Church, Episcopal, Bolinas

St. Aidan's Episcopal Church, Episcopal, San Francisco

St. Ambrose Episcopal Church, Episcopal, Foster City

St. Andrew's Episcopal Church, Episcopal, Saratoga

St. Augustine's Episcopal Church, Episcopal, Oakland

St. Clare's Episcopal Church, Episcopal, Pleasanton

St. Francis' Episcopal Church, Episcopal, San Francisco

St. James' Episcopal Church, Episcopal, San Francisco

St. John's Episcopal Church, Episcopal, Oakland

St. John-the-Evangelist Episcopal Church, Episcopal, San Francisco

St. Mark's Episcopal Church, Episcopal, Berkeley

St. Mark's Episcopal Church, Episcopal, Palo Alto

St. Peter's Episcopal Church, Episcopal, Redwood City

St. Peter's Episcopal Church, Episcopal, San Francisco

St. Stephen's Episcopal Church, Episcopal, Belvedere

St. Stephens In-the-Field Episcopal Church, Episcopal, San Jose

St. Thomas' Episcopal Church, Episcopal, Sunnyvale

Trinity Lutheran Church, Lutheran, Oakland

Trinity Presbyterian Church, Presbyterian, San Jose

INCENSE

Churches that use incense on a fairly regular basis in their main Sunday morning service.

All Saints' Episcopal Church, Episcopal, San Francisco

Church of the Advent of Christ the King, Episcopal, San Francisco

Church of the Holy Innocents, Episcopal, Corte Madera

Holy Innocents' Episcopal Church, Episcopal, San Francisco

St. Columba Episcopal Church, Episcopal, Inverness

St. Francis' Episcopal Church, Episcopal, San Francisco

St. John-the-Evangelist Episcopal Church, Episcopal, San Francisco

St. Luke's Episcopal Church, Episcopal, Los Gatos

Trinity Episcopal Church, Episcopal, San Francisco

Albany UMC, United Methodist Church, Albany

All Saints' Episcopal Church, Episcopal, San Francisco

Beth Eden Baptist Church, Baptist, Oakland

Bethany UMC, United Methodist Church, San Francisco

Calvary Presbyterian Church, Presbyterian, San Francisco

Chalice Christian Church, Disciples of Christ, San Mateo

Congregational Church of San Mateo, United Church of Christ, San Mateo

Episcopal Church of St. Mary the Virgin, Episcopal, San Francisco

First Baptist Church, Baptist, San Francisco

First Christian Church, Disciples of Christ, San Mateo

First Congregational Church, United Church of Christ, Berkeley

First Presbyterian Church, Presbyterian, Burlingame

First Presbyterian Church, Presbyterian, Milpitas

First Presbyterian Church of Palo Alto, Presbyterian, Palo Alto

New Creation Lutheran Church, Lutheran, San Jose

Ocean Avenue Presbyterian Church, Presbyterian, San Francisco

Presbyterian Church of Sunnyvale, Presbyterian, Sunnyvale

Redeemer Lutheran Church, Lutheran, Cupertino

Redwoods Presbyterian Church, Presbyterian, Larkspur

St. Aidan's Episcopal Church, Episcopal, San Francisco

St. Andrew's Episcopal Church, Episcopal, Saratoga

St. Clare's Episcopal Church, Episcopal, Pleasanton

St. James' Episcopal Church, Episcopal, San Francisco

St. Jude's Episcopal Church, Episcopal, Cupertino

St. Mark's Episcopal Church, Episcopal, Berkeley

St. Mark's Episcopal Church, Episcopal, Palo Alto

St. Stephen's Episcopal Church, Episcopal, Belvedere

St. Timothy's Episcopal Church, Episcopal, Mountain View

Seventh Avenue Presbyterian Church, Presbyterian, San Francisco

Trinity Episcopal Church, Episcopal, San Francisco

Trinity Presbyterian Church, Presbyterian, San Jose

Trinity UMC, United Methodist Church, Berkeley

University Lutheran Chapel, Lutheran, Berkeley

ATTRIBUTES OF INTEREST TO FAMILIES WITH CHILDREN

- *Youth or Christian Education Minister*
- *Junior Choir or Other Music Program for Children*
- *Big Sunday Schools*
- *Children Join the Congregation for the Entire Worship Service*
- *Regular Formal Programs for Teenagers*

YOUTH OR CHRISTIAN EDUCATION MINISTER

All Saints' Episcopal Church, Episcopal, Palo Alto

Almaden Valley UCC, United Church of Christ, San Jose

Asbury UMC, United Methodist Church, Livermore

Beth Eden Baptist Church, Baptist, Oakland

Bethel Community Presbyterian Church, Presbyterian, San Leandro

Calvary Presbyterian Church, Presbyterian, San Francisco

Christ Episcopal Church, Episcopal, Alameda

Christ Episcopal Church, Episcopal, Los Altos

Christ Presbyterian Church in Terra Linda, Presbyterian, San Rafael

Community Church of Mill Valley, United Church of Christ, Mill Valley

Community Congregational Church of Belvedere-Tiburon,
    United Church of Christ, Tiburon

Congregational Church of Belmont, United Church of Christ, Belmont

Congregational Church of San Mateo, United Church of Christ, San Mateo

Episcopal Church of the Incarnation, Episcopal, San Francisco

Episcopal Church of St. Mary the Virgin, Episcopal, San Francisco

First Baptist Church, Baptist, Oakland

First Baptist Church, Baptist, San Francisco

First Congregational Church, United Church of Christ, Berkeley

First Congregational UCC, United Church of Christ, Alameda

First Congregational UCC, United Church of Christ, San Jose

First Presbyterian Church, Presbyterian, Burlingame

First Presbyterian Church, Presbyterian, Milpitas

First Presbyterian Church, Presbyterian, Newark

First Presbyterian Church, Presbyterian, Oakland

First Presbyterian Church, Presbyterian, San Leandro

First Presbyterian Church, Presbyterian, Santa Clara

First Presbyterian Church of Mountain View, Presbyterian, Mountain View

First Presbyterian Church of Palo Alto, Presbyterian, Palo Alto

First UMC, United Methodist Church, Campbell

Fremont Congregational UCC, United Church of Christ, Fremont

Good Shepherd Episcopal Church, Episcopal, Belmont

Grace Lutheran Church, Lutheran, Palo Alto

Hillsdale United Methodist, United Methodist Church, San Mateo

Holy Trinity Lutheran Church, Lutheran, San Carlos

Hope Lutheran Church, Lutheran, El Sobrante

Immanuel Lutheran Church, Lutheran, San Jose

Ladera Community UCC, United Church of Christ, Portola Valley

Los Gatos UMC, United Methodist Church, Los Gatos

Lutheran Church of Our Savior, Lutheran, San Francisco

Marin Lutheran Church, Lutheran, Corte Madera

Melrose UMC, United Methodist Church, Oakland

Mira Vista UCC, United Church of Christ, El Cerrito

Morgan Hill United Methodist, United Methodist Church, Morgan Hill

Niles Congregational UCC, United Church of Christ, Fremont

Northminster Presbyterian Church, Presbyterian, El Cerrito

Presbyterian Church of Los Gatos, Presbyterian, Los Gatos

Presbyterian Church of Sunnyvale, Presbyterian, Sunnyvale

Resurrection Lutheran Church, Lutheran, Oakland

St. Aidan's Episcopal Church, Episcopal, San Francisco

St. Alban's Episcopal Church, Episcopal, Albany

St. Andrew's Episcopal Church, Episcopal, Saratoga

St. Augustine's Episcopal Church, Episcopal, Oakland

St. Clare's Episcopal Church, Episcopal, Pleasanton

St. Edmund's Episcopal Church, Episcopal, Pacifica

St. Francis' Episcopal Church, Episcopal, San Jose

St. Gregory of Nyssa Episcopal Church, Episcopal, San Francisco

St. James' Episcopal Church, Episcopal, San Francisco

St. John's Episcopal Church, Episcopal, Oakland

St. John's Episcopal Church, Episcopal, Ross

St. Joseph's Episcopal Church, Episcopal, Milpitas

St. Jude's Episcopal Church, Episcopal, Cupertino

St. Luke's Episcopal Church, Episcopal, Los Gatos

St. Mark's Episcopal Church, Episcopal, Berkeley

St. Mark's Episcopal Church, Episcopal, Palo Alto

St. Paul Lutheran Church, Lutheran, Oakland

St. Paul's Presbyterian Church, Presbyterian, San Francisco

St. Paul's UMC, United Methodist Church, San Jose

St. Stephen's Episcopal Church, Episcopal, Belvedere

St. Thomas' Episcopal Church, Episcopal, Sunnyvale

St. Timothy's Episcopal Church, Episcopal, Mountain View

San Lorenzo Community Church, United Church of Christ, San Lorenzo

Skyline Community UCC, United Church of Christ, Oakland

Sleepy Hollow Presbyterian Church, Presbyterian, San Anselmo

Trinity Lutheran Church, Lutheran, Alameda

Trinity Presbyterian Church, Presbyterian, San Jose

University Lutheran Chapel, Lutheran, Berkeley

West Valley Presbyterian Church, Presbyterian, Cupertino

All Saints' Episcopal Church, Episcopal, San Francisco

Almaden Valley UCC, United Church of Christ, San Jose

Asbury UMC, United Methodist Church, Livermore

Beth Eden Baptist Church, Baptist, Oakland

Bethany UMC, United Methodist Church, San Francisco

Calvary Presbyterian Church, Presbyterian, San Francisco

Christ Episcopal Church, Episcopal, Alameda

Christ the Good Shepherd Lutheran Church, Lutheran, San Jose

Christ the King Lutheran Church, Lutheran, Fremont

Christ Lutheran Church, Lutheran, San Francisco

Coastside Lutheran Church, Lutheran, Half Moon Bay

Community Congregational Church of Belvedere-Tiburon,
    United Church of Christ, Tiburon

Congregational Church of San Mateo, United Church of Christ, San Mateo

Covenant Presbyterian Church, Presbyterian, Palo Alto

Eden UCC, United Church of Christ, Hayward

Episcopal Church of St. Mary the Virgin, Episcopal, San Francisco

First Baptist Church, Baptist, Oakland

First Baptist Church, Baptist, San Francisco

First Congregational Church, United Church of Christ, Berkeley

First Congregational UCC, United Church of Christ, Alameda

First Congregational UCC, United Church of Christ, San Jose

First Presbyterian Church, Presbyterian, Burlingame

First Presbyterian Church, Presbyterian, Milpitas

First Presbyterian Church, Presbyterian, Newark

First Presbyterian Church of Mountain View, Presbyterian, Mountain View

First Presbyterian Church of Palo Alto, Presbyterian, Palo Alto

First UMC, United Methodist Church, Campbell

Fremont Congregational UCC, United Church of Christ, Fremont

Good Shepherd Episcopal Church, Episcopal, Belmont

Grace Lutheran Church, Lutheran, Palo Alto

Half Moon Bay Community UMC, United Methodist Church, Half Moon Bay

Hillsdale United Methodist, United Methodist Church, San Mateo

Holy Trinity Lutheran Church, Lutheran, San Carlos

Hope Lutheran Church, Lutheran, El Sobrante

Hope Lutheran Church, Lutheran, Santa Clara

Ingleside Presbyterian Church, Presbyterian, San Francisco

Ladera Community UCC, United Church of Christ, Portola Valley

Los Gatos UMC, United Methodist Church, Los Gatos

Marin Lutheran Church, Lutheran, Corte Madera

Morgan Hill United Methodist, United Methodist Church, Morgan Hill

New Creation Lutheran Church, Lutheran, San Jose

Niles Congregational UCC, United Church of Christ, Fremont

Northminster Presbyterian Church, Presbyterian, El Cerrito

Ocean Avenue Presbyterian Church, Presbyterian, San Francisco

Presbyterian Church of Los Gatos, Presbyterian, Los Gatos

Presbyterian Church of Sunnyvale, Presbyterian, Sunnyvale

Redwoods Presbyterian Church, Presbyterian, Larkspur

Resurrection Lutheran Church, Lutheran, Oakland

St. Ambrose Episcopal Church, Episcopal, Foster City

St. Andrew Presbyterian Church, Presbyterian, Pacifica

St. Andrew's Episcopal Church, Episcopal, Saratoga

St. Augustine's Episcopal Church, Episcopal, Oakland

St. Clement's Episcopal Church, Episcopal, Berkeley

St. Elizabeth's Episcopal Church, Episcopal, South San Francisco

St. Francis of Assisi Episcopal Church, Episcopal, Novato

St. James' Episcopal Church, Episcopal, San Francisco

St. John's Episcopal Church, Episcopal, Oakland

St. John's Episcopal Church, Episcopal, Ross

St. Luke's Episcopal Church, Episcopal, Los Gatos

St. Mark's Episcopal Church, Episcopal, Berkeley

St. Mark's Episcopal Church, Episcopal, Palo Alto

St. Paul Lutheran Church, Lutheran, Oakland

St. Peter's Episcopal Church, Episcopal, Redwood City

St. Stephen's Episcopal Church, Episcopal, Belvedere

St. Stephens In-the-Field Episcopal Church, Episcopal, San Jose

St. Timothy's Episcopal Church, Episcopal, Mountain View

San Martin Presbyterian Church, Presbyterian, San Martin

Skyline Community UCC, United Church of Christ, Oakland

Trinity Lutheran Church, Lutheran, Alameda

Valley Presbyterian Church, Presbyterian, Portola Valley

West Valley Presbyterian Church, Presbyterian, Cupertino

BIG SUNDAY SCHOOLS

These churches have big Sunday school programs, with either many classes or many children or both.

All Saints' Episcopal Church, Episcopal, Palo Alto

Asbury UMC, United Methodist Church, Livermore

Calvary Presbyterian Church, Presbyterian, San Francisco

Christ the King Lutheran Church, Lutheran, Fremont

Coastside Lutheran Church, Lutheran, Half Moon Bay

Congregational Church of San Mateo, United Church of Christ, San Mateo

Episcopal Church of St. Mary the Virgin, Episcopal, San Francisco

First Baptist Church, Baptist, Oakland

First Presbyterian Church, Presbyterian, Burlingame

First Congregational UCC, United Church of Christ, San Jose

First Presbyterian Church, Presbyterian, Milpitas

First Presbyterian Church, Presbyterian, Oakland

First Presbyterian Church of Mountain View, Presbyterian, Mountain View

First Presbyterian Church of Palo Alto, Presbyterian, Palo Alto

First UMC, United Methodist Church, Campbell

Los Gatos UMC, United Methodist Church, Los Gatos

Marin Lutheran Church, Lutheran, Corte Madera

Morgan Hill United Methodist, United Methodist Church, Morgan Hill

Presbyterian Church of Los Gatos, Presbyterian, Los Gatos

Presbyterian Church of Sunnyvale, Presbyterian, Sunnyvale

St. Andrew Presbyterian Church, Presbyterian, Pacifica

St. Andrew's Episcopal Church, Episcopal, Saratoga

St. Clement's Episcopal Church, Episcopal, Berkeley

St. James' Episcopal Church, Episcopal, San Francisco

St. John's Episcopal Church, Episcopal, Ross

St. Mark's Episcopal Church, Episcopal, Palo Alto

St. Stephen's Episcopal Church, Episcopal, Belvedere

Sleepy Hollow Presbyterian Church, Presbyterian, San Anselmo

West Valley Presbyterian Church, Presbyterian, Cupertino

CHILDREN JOIN THE CONGREGATION
FOR THE ENTIRE WORSHIP SERVICE

Bethany UMC, United Methodist Church, San Francisco

Bethel Community Presbyterian Church, Presbyterian, San Leandro

Chalice Christian Church, Disciples of Christ, San Mateo

Christ the Good Shepherd Lutheran Church, Lutheran, San Jose

Christ the King Lutheran Church, Lutheran, Fremont

Christ Lutheran Church, Lutheran, San Francisco

Christ the Victor Lutheran Church, Lutheran, Fairfax

Coastside Lutheran Church, Lutheran, Half Moon Bay

Congregational Church of Belmont, United Church of Christ, Belmont

Covenant Presbyterian Church, Presbyterian, Palo Alto

Faith Lutheran Church, Lutheran, San Rafael

First Baptist Church, Baptist, Oakland

First UMC, United Methodist Church, Campbell

Holy Innocents' Episcopal Church, Episcopal, San Francisco

Holy Redeemer Lutheran Church, Lutheran, San Jose

Holy Trinity Lutheran Church, Lutheran, San Carlos

Hope Lutheran Church, Lutheran, El Sobrante

Immanuel Lutheran Church, Lutheran, San Jose

Lincoln Park Presbyterian Church, Presbyterian, San Francisco

Lutheran Church of Our Savior, Lutheran, San Francisco

Marin Lutheran Church, Lutheran, Corte Madera

Messiah Lutheran Church, Lutheran, Redwood City

Mira Vista UCC, United Church of Christ, El Cerrito

Noe Valley Ministry, Presbyterian, San Francisco

Northminster Presbyterian Church, Presbyterian, El Cerrito

Peace Lutheran Church, Lutheran, San Bruno

Redeemer Lutheran Church, Lutheran, Cupertino

Resurrection Lutheran Church, Lutheran, Oakland

St. Andrew Presbyterian Church, Presbyterian, Pacifica

St. Columba Episcopal Church, Episcopal, Inverness

St. James' Episcopal Church, Episcopal, Fremont

St. James Lutheran Church, Lutheran, Richmond

St. Peter's Episcopal Church, Episcopal, San Francisco

St. Timothy's Episcopal Church, Episcopal, Mountain View

Sunnyhills UMC, United Methodist Church, Milpitas

Trinity Lutheran Church, Lutheran, Alameda

Trinity Lutheran Church, Lutheran, Oakland

Trinity Presbyterian Church, Presbyterian, San Jose

Trinity UMC, United Methodist Church, Berkeley

REGULAR FORMAL PROGRAMS FOR TEENAGERS

Almaden Valley UCC, United Church of Christ, San Jose

Asbury UMC, United Methodist Church, Livermore

Beth Eden Baptist Church, Baptist, Oakland

Bethel Community Presbyterian Church, Presbyterian, San Leandro

Broadmoor Presbyterian Church, Presbyterian, Daly City

Calvary Presbyterian Church, Presbyterian, San Francisco

Christ Episcopal Church, Episcopal, Alameda

Christ Episcopal Church, Episcopal, Los Altos

Christ Presbyterian Church in Terra Linda, Presbyterian, San Rafael

Community Congregational Church of Belvedere-Tiburon,
    United Church of Christ, Tiburon

Congregational Church of San Mateo, United Church of Christ, San Mateo

Covenant Presbyterian Church, Presbyterian, Palo Alto

Covenant Presbyterian Church, Presbyterian, San Francisco

Eden UCC, United Church of Christ, Hayward

Episcopal Church of the Incarnation, Episcopal, San Francisco

Episcopal Church of St. Mary the Virgin, Episcopal, San Francisco

First Baptist Church, Baptist, San Francisco

First Christian Church, Disciples of Christ, Palo Alto

First Congregational Church, United Church of Christ, Berkeley

First Congregational UCC, United Church of Christ, Alameda

First Congregational UCC, United Church of Christ, San Jose

First Presbyterian Church, Presbyterian, Milpitas

First Presbyterian Church, Presbyterian, Oakland

First Presbyterian Church, Presbyterian, San Leandro

First Presbyterian Church, Presbyterian, Santa Clara

First Presbyterian Church of Palo Alto, Presbyterian, Palo Alto

First UMC, United Methodist Church, Campbell

First UMC, United Methodist Church, San Rafael

Fremont Congregational UCC, United Church of Christ, Fremont

Half Moon Bay Community UMC, United Methodist Church, Half Moon Bay

Hillsdale United Methodist, United Methodist Church, San Mateo

Holy Cross Episcopal Church, Episcopal, Castro Valley

Holy Trinity Lutheran Church, Lutheran, San Carlos

Hope Lutheran Church, Lutheran, El Sobrante

Ingleside Presbyterian Church, Presbyterian, San Francisco

Ladera Community UCC, United Church of Christ, Portola Valley

Los Gatos UMC, United Methodist Church, Los Gatos

Lutheran Church of Our Savior, Lutheran, San Francisco

Marin Lutheran Church, Lutheran, Corte Madera

Mira Vista UCC, United Church of Christ, El Cerrito

Morgan Hill United Methodist, United Methodist Church, Morgan Hill

New Creation Lutheran Church, Lutheran, San Jose

Niles Congregational UCC, United Church of Christ, Fremont

Northminster Presbyterian Church, Presbyterian, El Cerrito

Ocean Avenue Presbyterian Church, Presbyterian, San Francisco

St. Aidan's Episcopal Church, Episcopal, San Francisco

St. Alban's Episcopal Church, Episcopal, Albany

St. Andrew's Episcopal Church, Episcopal, San Bruno

St. Augustine's Episcopal Church, Episcopal, Oakland

St. Clare's Episcopal Church, Episcopal, Pleasanton

St. Clement's Episcopal Church, Episcopal, Berkeley

St. Edmund's Episcopal Church, Episcopal, Pacifica

St. Francis of Assisi Episcopal Church, Episcopal, Novato

St. Francis' Episcopal Church, Episcopal, San Francisco

St. Francis' Episcopal Church, Episcopal, San Jose

St. Gregory of Nyssa Episcopal Church, Episcopal, San Francisco

St. James' Episcopal Church, Episcopal, Oakland

St. John's Episcopal Church, Episcopal, Oakland

St. Joseph's Episcopal Church, Episcopal, Milpitas

St. Jude's Episcopal Church, Episcopal, Cupertino

St. Mark's Episcopal Church, Episcopal, Berkeley

St. Mark's Episcopal Church, Episcopal, Palo Alto

St. Paul Lutheran Church, Lutheran, Oakland

St. Stephen's Episcopal Church, Episcopal, Belvedere

St. Stephens In-the-Field Episcopal Church, Episcopal, San Jose

St. Thomas' Episcopal Church, Episcopal, Sunnyvale

St. Timothy's Episcopal Church, Episcopal, Mountain View

San Lorenzo Community Church, United Church of Christ, San Lorenzo

San Martin Presbyterian Church, Presbyterian, San Martin

Sleepy Hollow Presbyterian Church, Presbyterian, San Anselmo

South Berkeley Community Church, United Church of Christ, Berkeley

Sunset Ministry, Baptist, San Francisco

Trinity Lutheran Church, Lutheran, Alameda

Trinity Presbyterian Church, Presbyterian, San Jose

United Methodist Church of Daly City, United Methodist Church, Daly City

University Lutheran Chapel, Lutheran, Berkeley

Valley Presbyterian Church, Presbyterian, Portola Valley

West Valley Presbyterian Church, Presbyterian, Cupertino

ATTRIBUTES OF INTEREST TO LESBIANS, GAYS, BISEXUALS, AND TRANSGENDERED INDIVIDUALS

- *Affiliated with an LGBT advocacy group*
- *Parish Mission Statement Includes the Words "Inclusive" or "Welcoming"*
- *Same-Sex Blessings*

AFFILIATED WITH AN LGBT ADVOCACY GROUP

Albany UMC, United Methodist Church, Albany

All Saints' Episcopal Church, Episcopal, Palo Alto

Alum Rock UMC, United Methodist Church, San Jose

Bethany UMC, United Methodist Church, San Francisco

Chalice Christian Church, Disciples of Christ, San Mateo

Christ the Good Shepherd Lutheran Church, Lutheran, San Jose

Christ Lutheran Church, Lutheran, San Francisco

Christ Presbyterian Church in Terra Linda, Presbyterian, San Rafael

Christ the Victor Lutheran Church, Lutheran, Fairfax

Church of the Advent of Christ the King, Episcopal, San Francisco

College Heights Church, United Church of Christ, San Mateo

Community Congregational Church of Belvedere-Tiburon,
    United Church of Christ, Tiburon

Congregational Church of Belmont, United Church of Christ, Belmont

Eden UCC, United Church of Christ, Hayward

Episcopal Church of the Incarnation, Episcopal, San Francisco

Fairfax Community Church, United Church of Christ, Fairfax

Faith Lutheran Church, Lutheran, San Rafael

First Christian Church, Disciples of Christ, San Mateo

First Congregational Church, United Church of Christ, Berkeley

First Congregational UCC, United Church of Christ, Alameda

First Congregational UCC, United Church of Christ, Oakland

First Congregational UCC, United Church of Christ, San Jose

First Presbyterian Church of Palo Alto, Presbyterian, Palo Alto

First UMC, United Methodist Church, Campbell

First UMC, United Methodist Church, San Rafael

Fremont Congregational UCC, United Church of Christ, Fremont

Good Shepherd Episcopal Church, Episcopal, Belmont

Grace UMC of Saratoga, United Methodist Church, Saratoga

Hillsdale United Methodist, United Methodist Church, San Mateo

Holy Redeemer Lutheran Church, Lutheran, San Jose

Immanuel Lutheran Church, Lutheran, San Jose

Ladera Community UCC, United Church of Christ, Portola Valley

Lake Merritt UMC, United Methodist Church, Oakland

Lutheran Church of Our Savior, Lutheran, San Francisco

Marin Lutheran Church, Lutheran, Corte Madera

Mira Vista UCC, United Church of Christ, El Cerrito

Morgan Hill United Methodist, United Methodist Church, Morgan Hill

Niles Congregational UCC, United Church of Christ, Fremont

Noe Valley Ministry, Presbyterian, San Francisco

Northminster Presbyterian Church, Presbyterian, El Cerrito

Ocean Avenue Presbyterian Church, Presbyterian, San Francisco

Peace Lutheran Church, Lutheran, San Bruno

Redeemer Lutheran Church, Lutheran, Cupertino

Redwoods Presbyterian Church, Presbyterian, Larkspur

St. Aidan's Episcopal Church, Episcopal, San Francisco

St. Edmund's Episcopal Church, Episcopal, Pacifica

St. James' Episcopal Church, Episcopal, San Francisco

St. John-the-Evangelist Episcopal Church, Episcopal, San Francisco

St. Johns UCC, United Church of Christ, San Francisco

St. Joseph's Episcopal Church, Episcopal, Milpitas

St. Jude's Episcopal Church, Episcopal, Cupertino

St. Luke's Episcopal Church, Episcopal, Los Gatos

St. Mark's Episcopal Church, Episcopal, Berkeley

St. Mark's Episcopal Church, Episcopal, Palo Alto

St. Paul Lutheran Church, Lutheran, Oakland

St. Paul's UMC, United Methodist Church, San Jose

St. Peter's Episcopal Church, Episcopal, Redwood City

St. Stephen's Episcopal Church, Episcopal, Belvedere

St. Stephens In-the-Field Episcopal Church, Episcopal, San Jose

St. Thomas' Episcopal Church, Episcopal, Sunnyvale

San Leandro Community Church, Baptist, San Leandro

San Martin Presbyterian Church, Presbyterian, San Martin

Seventh Avenue Presbyterian Church, Presbyterian, San Francisco

Sunnyhills UMC, United Methodist Church, Milpitas

Trinity Episcopal Church, Episcopal, San Francisco

Trinity Lutheran Church, Lutheran, Alameda

Trinity Lutheran Church, Lutheran, Oakland

Trinity UMC, United Methodist Church, Berkeley

United Methodist Church of Daly City, United Methodist Church, Daly City

University Lutheran Chapel, Lutheran, Berkeley

All Saints' Episcopal Church, Episcopal, San Francisco

PARISH MISSION STATEMENT INCLUDES THE WORDS "INCLUSIVE" OR "WELCOMING"

Albany UMC, United Methodist Church, Albany

All Saints' Episcopal Church, Episcopal, Palo Alto

All Saints' Episcopal Church, Episcopal, San Francisco

Alum Rock UMC, United Methodist Church, San Jose

Bethany UMC, United Methodist Church, San Francisco

Chalice Christian Church, Disciples of Christ, San Mateo

Christ Episcopal Church, Episcopal, Los Altos

Christ the Good Shepherd Lutheran Church, Lutheran, San Jose

Christ the King Lutheran Church, Lutheran, Fremont

Christ Lutheran Church, Lutheran, San Francisco

College Heights Church, United Church of Christ, San Mateo

Community Congregational Church of Belvedere-Tiburon,
    United Church of Christ, Tiburon

Congregational Church of Belmont, United Church of Christ, Belmont

Congregational Church of San Mateo, United Church of Christ, San Mateo

Covenant Presbyterian Church, Presbyterian, San Francisco

Eden UCC, United Church of Christ, Hayward

Episcopal Church of the Incarnation, Episcopal, San Francisco

Episcopal Church of St. Mary the Virgin, Episcopal, San Francisco

Fairfax Community Church, United Church of Christ, Fairfax

First Christian Church, Disciples of Christ, San Mateo

First Congregational Church, United Church of Christ, Berkeley

First Congregational UCC, United Church of Christ, Alameda

First Congregational UCC, United Church of Christ, Oakland

First Congregational UCC, United Church of Christ, San Jose

First UMC, United Methodist Church, Campbell

First UMC, United Methodist Church, San Rafael

Fremont Congregational UCC, United Church of Christ, Fremont

Grace Lutheran Church, Lutheran, Palo Alto

Grace UMC of Saratoga, United Methodist Church, Saratoga

Hillsdale United Methodist, United Methodist Church, San Mateo

Hope Lutheran Church, Lutheran, El Sobrante

Immanuel Lutheran Church, Lutheran, San Jose

Ladera Community UCC, United Church of Christ, Portola Valley

Los Gatos UMC, United Methodist Church, Los Gatos

Lutheran Church of Our Savior, Lutheran, San Francisco

Marin Lutheran Church, Lutheran, Corte Madera

Melrose UMC, United Methodist Church, Oakland

Morgan Hill United Methodist, United Methodist Church, Morgan Hill

New Creation Lutheran Church, Lutheran, San Jose

Mira Vista UCC, United Church of Christ, El Cerrito

Niles Congregational UCC, United Church of Christ, Fremont

Noe Valley Ministry, Presbyterian, San Francisco

Peace Lutheran Church, Lutheran, San Bruno

Plymouth UCC, United Church of Christ, Oakland

St. Aidan's Episcopal Church, Episcopal, Bolinas

St. Aidan's Episcopal Church, Episcopal, San Francisco

St. Ambrose Episcopal Church, Episcopal, Foster City

St. Andrew Presbyterian Church, Presbyterian, Pacifica

St. Andrew's Episcopal Church, Episcopal, San Bruno

St. Andrew's Episcopal Church, Episcopal, Saratoga

St. Edmund's Episcopal Church, Episcopal, Pacifica

St. Elizabeth's Episcopal Church, Episcopal, South San Francisco

St. Francis' Episcopal Church, Episcopal, San Francisco

St. Gregory of Nyssa Episcopal Church, Episcopal, San Francisco

St. James' Episcopal Church, Episcopal, Fremont

St. Johns UCC, United Church of Christ, San Francisco

St. Joseph's Episcopal Church, Episcopal, Milpitas

St. Jude's Episcopal Church, Episcopal, Cupertino

St. Luke's Episcopal Church, Episcopal, Los Gatos

St. Mark's Episcopal Church, Episcopal, Berkeley

St. Mark's Episcopal Church, Episcopal, Palo Alto

St. Paul Lutheran Church, Lutheran, Oakland

St. Paul's UMC, United Methodist Church, San Jose

St. Peter's Episcopal Church, Episcopal, Redwood City

St. Stephen's Episcopal Church, Episcopal, Belvedere

St. Stephens In-the-Field Episcopal Church, Episcopal, San Jose

St. Thomas' Episcopal Church, Episcopal, Sunnyvale

San Leandro Community Church, Baptist, San Leandro

Skyline Community UCC, United Church of Christ, Oakland

Sunnyhills UMC, United Methodist Church, Milpitas

Trinity Episcopal Church, Episcopal, San Francisco

Trinity Lutheran Church, Lutheran, Alameda

Trinity Lutheran Church, Lutheran, Oakland

Trinity UMC, United Methodist Church, Berkeley

United Methodist Church of Daly City, United Methodist Church, Daly City

University Lutheran Chapel, Lutheran, Berkeley

SAME-SEX BLESSINGS

These churches have indicated that they bless same-sex unions or, if the climate of their national church prohibits union ceremonies, that they offer an alternative to same-sex couples.

All Saints' Episcopal Church, Episcopal, Palo Alto

All Saints' Episcopal Church, Episcopal, San Francisco

Alum Rock UMC, United Methodist Church, San Jose

Broadmoor Presbyterian Church, Presbyterian, Daly City

Calvary Presbyterian Church, Presbyterian, San Francisco

Chalice Christian Church, Disciples of Christ, San Mateo

Christ Episcopal Church, Episcopal, Alameda

Christ Episcopal Church, Episcopal, Los Altos

Christ Lutheran Church, Lutheran, San Francisco

Christ Presbyterian Church in Terra Linda, Presbyterian, San Rafael

Christ the Victor Lutheran Church, Lutheran, Fairfax

Church of the Advent of Christ the King, Episcopal, San Francisco

College Heights Church, United Church of Christ, San Mateo

Community Church of Mill Valley, United Church of Christ, Mill Valley

Community Congregational Church of Belvedere-Tiburon,
    United Church of Christ, Tiburon

Congregational Church of Belmont, United Church of Christ, Belmont

Congregational Church of San Mateo, United Church of Christ, San Mateo

Covenant Presbyterian Church, Presbyterian, San Francisco

Episcopal Church of the Incarnation, Episcopal, San Francisco

Fairfax Community Church, United Church of Christ, Fairfax

Faith Lutheran Church, Lutheran, San Rafael

First Christian Church, Disciples of Christ, San Mateo

First Congregational Church, United Church of Christ, Berkeley

First Congregational UCC, United Church of Christ, Alameda

First Congregational UCC, United Church of Christ, Oakland

First Congregational UCC, United Church of Christ, San Jose

First Presbyterian Church of Palo Alto, Presbyterian, Palo Alto

First UMC, United Methodist Church, San Rafael

Fremont Congregational UCC, United Church of Christ, Fremont

Good Shepherd Episcopal Church, Episcopal, Belmont

Holy Cross Episcopal Church, Episcopal, Castro Valley

Holy Innocents' Episcopal Church, Episcopal, San Francisco

Holy Redeemer Lutheran Church, Lutheran, San Jose

Immanuel Lutheran Church, Lutheran, San Jose

Ladera Community UCC, United Church of Christ, Portola Valley

Lake Merritt UMC, United Methodist Church, Oakland

Lutheran Church of Our Savior, Lutheran, San Francisco

Messiah Lutheran Church, Lutheran, Redwood City

Mira Vista UCC, United Church of Christ, El Cerrito

Morgan Hill United Methodist, United Methodist Church, Morgan Hill

Niles Congregational UCC, United Church of Christ, Fremont

Noe Valley Ministry, Presbyterian, San Francisco

Northminster Presbyterian Church, Presbyterian, El Cerrito

Ocean Avenue Presbyterian Church, Presbyterian, San Francisco

Peace Lutheran Church, Lutheran, San Bruno

Plymouth UCC, United Church of Christ, Oakland

Redeemer Lutheran Church, Lutheran, Cupertino

Redwoods Presbyterian Church, Presbyterian, Larkspur

Resurrection Lutheran Church, Lutheran, Oakland

St. Aidan's Episcopal Church, Episcopal, Bolinas

St. Aidan's Episcopal Church, Episcopal, San Francisco

St. Andrew's Episcopal Church, Episcopal, Saratoga

St. Clare's Episcopal Church, Episcopal, Pleasanton

St. Edmund's Episcopal Church, Episcopal, Pacifica

St. Francis' Episcopal Church, Episcopal, San Francisco

St. Gregory of Nyssa Episcopal Church, Episcopal, San Francisco

St. James' Episcopal Church, Episcopal, San Francisco

St. John-the-Evangelist Episcopal Church, Episcopal, San Francisco

St. Johns UCC, United Church of Christ, San Francisco

St. Joseph's Episcopal Church, Episcopal, Milpitas

St. Jude's Episcopal Church, Episcopal, Cupertino

St. Luke's Episcopal Church, Episcopal, Los Gatos

St. Mark's Episcopal Church, Episcopal, Berkeley

St. Mark's Episcopal Church, Episcopal, Palo Alto

St. Paul Lutheran Church, Lutheran, Oakland

St. Peter's Episcopal Church, Episcopal, Redwood City

St. Peter's Episcopal Church, Episcopal, San Francisco

St. Stephen's Episcopal Church, Episcopal, Belvedere

St. Thomas' Episcopal Church, Episcopal, Sunnyvale

San Leandro Community Church, Baptist, San Leandro

San Lorenzo Community Church, United Church of Christ, San Lorenzo

Seventh Avenue Presbyterian Church, Presbyterian, San Francisco

Skyline Community UCC, United Church of Christ, Oakland

Trinity Episcopal Church, Episcopal, San Francisco

Trinity Lutheran Church, Lutheran, Oakland

Trinity UMC, United Methodist Church, Berkeley

University Lutheran Chapel, Lutheran, Berkeley

ATTRIBUTES OF INTEREST TO CULTURAL CREATIVES/POLITICAL PROGRESSIVES

- *Pastor Called by His or Her First Name*
- *Inclusive Language Is a Top Priority*
- *Female Lead Clergy*
- *Innovative or Creative Liturgical Style*
- *Nontraditional Instrumentation Used in Worship Services*
- *Nontraditional Texts Used in Worship Services*
- *Liturgical Dance Used in Worship Services*
- *Original Music or Liturgical Texts Created by Music Staff or Members of the Congregation Other Creative or Unusual Elements Used Regularly in Worship Services*
- *Affiliated with Center for Progressive Christianity*
- *Unofficial Dress Code Is "Play Clothes" Casual*
- *Same-Sex Blessings*
- *Parish Mission Statement Includes the Words "Inclusive" or "Welcoming"*
- *Alternative Services*

PASTOR CALLED BY HIS OR HER FIRST NAME

All Saints' Episcopal Church, Episcopal, Palo Alto

All Saints' Episcopal Church, Episcopal, San Francisco

Almaden Valley UCC, United Church of Christ, San Jose

Alum Rock UMC, United Methodist Church, San Jose

Asbury UMC, United Methodist Church, Livermore

Bethany UMC, United Methodist Church, San Francisco

Bethel Community Presbyterian Church, Presbyterian, San Leandro

Chalice Christian Church, Disciples of Christ, San Mateo

Christ Episcopal Church, Episcopal, Alameda

Christ Episcopal Church, Episcopal, Los Altos

Christ Episcopal Church, Episcopal, Sausalito

Christ Presbyterian Church in Terra Linda, Presbyterian, San Rafael

College Heights Church, United Church of Christ, San Mateo

Community Church of Mill Valley, United Church of Christ, Mill Valley

Community Congregational Church of Belvedere-Tiburon,
    United Church of Christ, Tiburon

Congregational Church of Belmont, United Church of Christ, Belmont

Congregational Church of San Mateo, United Church of Christ, San Mateo

Eden UCC, United Church of Christ, Hayward

Episcopal Church of the Incarnation, Episcopal, San Francisco

Fairfax Community Church, United Church of Christ, Fairfax

First Baptist Church, Baptist, Oakland

First Baptist Church, Baptist, San Francisco

First Christian Church, Disciples of Christ, Palo Alto

First Christian Church, Disciples of Christ, San Mateo

First Congregational Church, United Church of Christ, Berkeley

First Congregational UCC, United Church of Christ, Alameda

First Congregational UCC, United Church of Christ, Oakland

First Congregational UCC, United Church of Christ, San Jose

First Presbyterian Church, Presbyterian, Burlingame

First Presbyterian Church, Presbyterian, Santa Clara

First Presbyterian Church of Mountain View, Presbyterian, Mountain View

First Presbyterian Church of Palo Alto, Presbyterian, Palo Alto

First UMC, United Methodist Church, San Rafael

Fremont Congregational UCC, United Church of Christ, Fremont

Good Shepherd Episcopal Church, Episcopal, Belmont

Grace UMC of Saratoga, United Methodist Church, Saratoga

Hillsdale United Methodist, United Methodist Church, San Mateo

Holy Cross Episcopal Church, Episcopal, Castro Valley

Holy Innocents' Episcopal Church, Episcopal, San Francisco

Ladera Community UCC, United Church of Christ, Portola Valley

Lincoln Park Presbyterian Church, Presbyterian, San Francisco

New Life Church, Baptist, Richmond

New Spirit Community Church, United Church of Christ, Berkeley

Niles Congregational UCC, United Church of Christ, Fremont

Noe Valley Ministry, Presbyterian, San Francisco

Northminster Presbyterian Church, Presbyterian, El Cerrito

Plymouth UCC, United Church of Christ, Oakland

Presbyterian Church of Los Gatos, Presbyterian, Los Gatos

Presbyterian Church of Sunnyvale, Presbyterian, Sunnyvale

St. Alban's Episcopal Church, Episcopal, Albany

St. Aidan's Episcopal Church, Episcopal, San Francisco

St. Ambrose Episcopal Church, Episcopal, Foster City

St. Andrew Presbyterian Church, Presbyterian, Pacifica

St. Andrew's Episcopal Church, Episcopal, Saratoga

St. Edmund's Episcopal Church, Episcopal, Pacifica

St. Elizabeth's Episcopal Church, Episcopal, South San Francisco

St. Francis' Episcopal Church, Episcopal, San Francisco

St. Francis' Episcopal Church, Episcopal, San Jose

St. Gregory of Nyssa Episcopal Church, Episcopal, San Francisco

St. James' Episcopal Church, Episcopal, Fremont

St. James' Episcopal Church, Episcopal, San Francisco

St. John's Episcopal Church, Episcopal, Oakland

St. John-the-Evangelist Episcopal Church, Episcopal, San Francisco

St. Johns UCC, United Church of Christ, San Francisco

St. Mark's Episcopal Church, Episcopal, Berkeley

St. Mark's Episcopal Church, Episcopal, Palo Alto

St. Paul's Presbyterian Church, Presbyterian, San Francisco

St. Timothy's Episcopal Church, Episcopal, Mountain View

San Lorenzo Community Church, United Church of Christ, San Lorenzo

Seventh Avenue Presbyterian Church, Presbyterian, San Francisco

Sunnyhills UMC, United Methodist Church, Milpitas

Trinity UMC, United Methodist Church, Berkeley

INCLUSIVE LANGUAGE IS A TOP PRIORITY

All Saints' Episcopal Church, Episcopal, San Francisco

Almaden Valley UCC, United Church of Christ, San Jose

Bethel Community Presbyterian Church, Presbyterian, San Leandro

Beth Eden Baptist Church, Baptist, Oakland

Broadmoor Presbyterian Church, Presbyterian, Daly City

Calvary Presbyterian Church, Presbyterian, San Francisco

Chalice Christian Church, Disciples of Christ, San Mateo

Christ Episcopal Church, Episcopal, Alameda

Christ Episcopal Church, Episcopal, Los Altos

Christ the Good Shepherd Lutheran Church, Lutheran, San Jose

Christ Presbyterian Church in Terra Linda, Presbyterian, San Rafael

College Heights Church, United Church of Christ, San Mateo

Community Church of Mill Valley, United Church of Christ, Mill Valley

Community Congregational Church of Belvedere-Tiburon,
      United Church of Christ, Tiburon

Congregational Church of Belmont, United Church of Christ, Belmont

Fairfax Community Church, United Church of Christ, Fairfax

Faith Lutheran Church, Lutheran, San Rafael

First Baptist Church, Baptist, Oakland

First Christian Church, Disciples of Christ, Palo Alto

First Congregational Church, United Church of Christ, Berkeley

First Congregational UCC, United Church of Christ, Alameda

First Congregational UCC, United Church of Christ, Oakland

First Presbyterian Church, Presbyterian, San Leandro

First Presbyterian Church of Palo Alto, Presbyterian, Palo Alto

First UMC, United Methodist Church, Campbell

Fremont Congregational UCC, United Church of Christ, Fremont

Good Shepherd Episcopal Church, Episcopal, Belmont

Hillsdale United Methodist, United Methodist Church, San Mateo

Holy Innocents' Episcopal Church, Episcopal, San Francisco

Hope Lutheran Church, Lutheran, Santa Clara

Ladera Community UCC, United Church of Christ, Portola Valley

Lincoln Park Presbyterian Church, Presbyterian, San Francisco

Los Gatos UMC, United Methodist Church, Los Gatos

Lutheran Church of Our Savior, Lutheran, San Francisco

Melrose UMC, United Methodist Church, Oakland

Mira Vista UCC, United Church of Christ, El Cerrito

Morgan Hill United Methodist, United Methodist Church, Morgan Hill

New Creation Lutheran Church, Lutheran, San Jose

New Spirit Community Church, United Church of Christ, Berkeley

Noe Valley Ministry, Presbyterian, San Francisco

Ocean Avenue Presbyterian Church, Presbyterian, San Francisco

Plymouth UCC, United Church of Christ, Oakland

Presbyterian Church of Los Gatos, Presbyterian, Los Gatos

Presbyterian Church of Sunnyvale, Presbyterian, Sunnyvale

Redeemer Lutheran Church, Lutheran, Cupertino

Redwoods Presbyterian Church, Presbyterian, Larkspur

Resurrection Lutheran Church, Lutheran, Oakland

St. Aidan's Episcopal Church, Episcopal, Bolinas

St. Aidan's Episcopal Church, Episcopal, San Francisco

St. Alban's Episcopal Church, Episcopal, Albany

St. Andrew Presbyterian Church, Presbyterian, Pacifica

St. Augustine's Episcopal Church, Episcopal, Oakland

St. Edmund's Episcopal Church, Episcopal, Pacifica

St. Gregory of Nyssa Episcopal Church, Episcopal, San Francisco

St. James' Episcopal Church, Episcopal, San Francisco

St. John's Episcopal Church, Episcopal, Oakland

St. John-the-Evangelist Episcopal Church, Episcopal, San Francisco

St. Philip's Episcopal Church, Episcopal, San Jose

St. Stephens In-the-Field Episcopal Church, Episcopal, San Jose

San Leandro Community Church, Baptist, San Leandro

Seventh Avenue Presbyterian Church, Presbyterian, San Francisco

Trinity Lutheran Church, Lutheran, Alameda

Trinity Lutheran Church, Lutheran, Oakland

United Methodist Church of Daly City, United Methodist Church, Daly City

University Lutheran Chapel, Lutheran, Berkeley

FEMALE LEAD CLERGY

Includes congregations having male/female teams, including couples.

Albany UMC, United Methodist Church, Albany

All Saints' Episcopal Church, Episcopal, Palo Alto

Almaden Valley UCC, United Church of Christ, San Jose

Alum Rock UMC, United Methodist Church, San Jose

Bethany UMC, United Methodist Church, San Francisco

Bethel Community Presbyterian Church, Presbyterian, San Leandro

Broadmoor Presbyterian Church, Presbyterian, Daly City

Christ Episcopal Church, Episcopal, Los Altos

Coastside Lutheran Church, Lutheran, Half Moon Bay

Community Church of Mill Valley, United Church of Christ, Mill Valley

Community Congregational Church of Belvedere-Tiburon,
    United Church of Christ, Tiburon

Congregational Church of Belmont, United Church of Christ, Belmont

Fairfax Community Church, United Church of Christ, Fairfax

First Congregational Church, United Church of Christ, Berkeley

First Presbyterian Church, Presbyterian, San Leandro

First UMC, United Methodist Church, Campbell

Fremont Congregational UCC, United Church of Christ, Fremont

Grace UMC of Saratoga, United Methodist Church, Saratoga

Hillsdale United Methodist, United Methodist Church, San Mateo

Holy Innocents' Episcopal Church, Episcopal, San Francisco

Holy Trinity Lutheran Church, Lutheran, San Carlos

Immanuel Lutheran Church, Lutheran, San Jose

Lake Merritt UMC, United Methodist Church, Oakland

Los Gatos UMC, United Methodist Church, Los Gatos

Marin Lutheran Church, Lutheran, Corte Madera

Messiah Lutheran Church, Lutheran, Redwood City

Mira Vista UCC, United Church of Christ, El Cerrito

New Life Church, Baptist, Richmond

New Spirit Community Church, United Church of Christ, Berkeley

Noe Valley Ministry, Presbyterian, San Francisco

Northminster Presbyterian Church, Presbyterian, El Cerrito

Ocean Avenue Presbyterian Church, Presbyterian, San Francisco

Peace Lutheran Church, Lutheran, San Bruno

Plymouth UCC, United Church of Christ, Oakland

Redeemer Lutheran Church, Lutheran, Cupertino

Redwoods Presbyterian Church, Presbyterian, Larkspur

Resurrection Lutheran Church, Lutheran, Oakland

St. Aidan's Episcopal Church, Episcopal, San Francisco

St. Andrew Presbyterian Church, Presbyterian, Pacifica

St. Andrew's Episcopal Church, Episcopal, San Bruno

St. Augustine's Episcopal Church, Episcopal, Oakland

St. Elizabeth's Episcopal Church, Episcopal, South San Francisco

St. James' Episcopal Church, Episcopal, Fremont

St. James' Episcopal Church, Episcopal, San Francisco

St. Jude's Episcopal Church, Episcopal, Cupertino

St. Mark's Episcopal Church, Episcopal, Berkeley

St. Stephens In-the-Field Episcopal Church, Episcopal, San Jose

St. Thomas' Episcopal Church, Episcopal, Sunnyvale

San Leandro Community Church, Baptist, San Leandro

Sleepy Hollow Presbyterian Church, Presbyterian, San Anselmo

South Berkeley Community Church, United Church of Christ, Berkeley

Sunnyhills UMC, United Methodist Church, Milpitas

Trinity Lutheran Church, Lutheran, Alameda

Trinity Lutheran Church, Lutheran, Oakland

Trinity UMC, United Methodist Church, Berkeley

INNOVATIVE OR CREATIVE LITURGICAL STYLE

Churches were asked to choose which of the following four phrases most accurately describe their liturgical style: Traditional, Evangelical, Charismatic, Innovative/Experimental. Congregations on this list chose Innovative/Experimental.

Asbury UMC, United Methodist Church, Livermore

Bethany UMC, United Methodist Church, San Francisco

Bethel Community Presbyterian Church, Presbyterian, San Leandro

Chalice Christian Church, Disciples of Christ, San Mateo

College Heights Church, United Church of Christ, San Mateo

Community Congregational Church of Belvedere-Tiburon,
    United Church of Christ, Tiburon

Congregational Church of Belmont, United Church of Christ, Belmont

Episcopal Church of St. Mary the Virgin, Episcopal, San Francisco

Fairfax Community Church, United Church of Christ, Fairfax

First Christian Church, Disciples of Christ, San Mateo

First Congregational Church, United Church of Christ, Berkeley

First UMC, United Methodist Church, San Rafael

Good Shepherd Episcopal Church, Episcopal, Belmont

Holy Redeemer Lutheran Church, Lutheran, San Jose

Immanuel Lutheran Church, Lutheran, San Jose

Lake Merritt UMC, United Methodist Church, Oakland

Melrose UMC, United Methodist Church, Oakland

Mira Vista UCC, United Church of Christ, El Cerrito

Morgan Hill United Methodist, United Methodist Church, Morgan Hill

New Life Church, Baptist, Richmond

New Spirit Community Church, United Church of Christ, Berkeley

Redeemer Lutheran Church, Lutheran, Cupertino

St. Aidan's Episcopal Church, Episcopal, San Francisco

St. Andrew's Episcopal Church, Episcopal, San BrunoSt. Elizabeth's Episcopal
Church, Episcopal, South San Francisco

St. Gregory of Nyssa Episcopal Church, Episcopal, San Francisco

St. James' Episcopal Church, Episcopal, San Francisco

St. Stephen's Episcopal Church, Episcopal, Belvedere

St. Timothy's Episcopal Church, Episcopal, Mountain View

San Leandro Community Church, Baptist, San Leandro

Seventh Avenue Presbyterian Church, Presbyterian, San Francisco

Trinity Lutheran Church, Lutheran, Oakland

University Lutheran Chapel, Lutheran, Berkeley

NONTRADITIONAL INSTRUMENTATION USED IN WORSHIP SERVICES

Churches on this list regularly use instruments other than an organ or piano as the primary instrumentation.

Asbury UMC, United Methodist Church, Livermore

Bethany UMC, United Methodist Church, San Francisco

Christ Lutheran Church, Lutheran, San Francisco

Christ the Victor Lutheran Church, Lutheran, Fairfax

Covenant Presbyterian Church, Presbyterian, San Francisco

First Presbyterian Church, Presbyterian, Milpitas

Grace UMC of Saratoga, United Methodist Church, Saratoga

Lake Merritt UMC, United Methodist Church, Oakland

Los Gatos UMC, United Methodist Church, Los Gatos

Lutheran Church of Our Savior, Lutheran, San Francisco

Morgan Hill United Methodist, United Methodist Church, Morgan Hill

New Creation Lutheran Church, Lutheran, San Jose

Noe Valley Ministry, Presbyterian, San Francisco

Redeemer Lutheran Church, Lutheran, Cupertino

St. Andrew Presbyterian Church, Presbyterian, Pacifica

St. Augustine's Episcopal Church, Episcopal, Oakland

St. Columba Episcopal Church, Episcopal, Inverness

St. Elizabeth's Episcopal Church, Episcopal, South San Francisco

St. Gregory of Nyssa Episcopal Church, Episcopal, San Francisco

St. James' Episcopal Church, Episcopal, Oakland

St. Jude's Episcopal Church, Episcopal, Cupertino

St. Peter's Episcopal Church, Episcopal, San Francisco

St. Philip's Episcopal Church, Episcopal, San Jose

St. Timothy's Episcopal Church, Episcopal, Mountain View

Seventh Avenue Presbyterian Church, Presbyterian, San Francisco

Sleepy Hollow Presbyterian Church, Presbyterian, San Anselmo

Sunset Ministry, Baptist, San Francisco

Trinity Lutheran Church, Lutheran, Alameda

Trinity Lutheran Church, Lutheran, Oakland

Trinity UMC, United Methodist Church, Berkeley

NONTRADITIONAL TEXTS USED IN WORSHIP SERVICES

College Heights Church, United Church of Christ, San Mateo

Community Congregational Church of Belvedere-Tiburon,
    United Church of Christ, Tiburon

Fairfax Community Church, United Church of Christ, Fairfax

First Baptist Church, Baptist, Oakland

First Congregational Church, United Church of Christ, Berkeley

First Congregational UCC, United Church of Christ, Alameda

First UMC, United Methodist Church, San Rafael

Grace UMC of Saratoga, United Methodist Church, Saratoga

Ladera Community UCC, United Church of Christ, Portola Valley

Lutheran Church of Our Savior, Lutheran, San Francisco

Morgan Hill United Methodist, United Methodist Church, Morgan Hill

New Life Church, Baptist, Richmond

Noe Valley Ministry, Presbyterian, San Francisco

Plymouth UCC, United Church of Christ, Oakland

Redeemer Lutheran Church, Lutheran, Cupertino

Resurrection Lutheran Church, Lutheran, Oakland

St. Aidan's Episcopal Church, Episcopal, San Francisco

St. Gregory of Nyssa Episcopal Church, Episcopal, San Francisco

LITURGICAL DANCE USED IN WORSHIP SERVICES

While many churches might incorporate dance into their liturgy once in a while, these congregations have indicated that they get up and dance together on a regular basis.

Asbury United Methodist Church, United Methodist Church, Livermore

Beth Eden Baptist Church, Baptist, Oakland

College Heights Church, United Church of Christ, San Mateo

Congregational Church of Belmont, United Church of Christ, Belmont

First Congregational Church, United Church of Christ, Berkeley

First Congregational UCC, United Church of Christ, Alameda

First Presbyterian Church, Presbyterian, Burlingame

First United Methodist Church, United Methodist Church, San Rafael

Grace United Methodist Church of Saratoga, United Methodist Church, Saratoga

New Life Church, Baptist, Richmond

New Spirit Community Church, United Church of Christ, Berkeley

Seventh Avenue Presbyterian Church, Presbyterian, San Francisco

Sleepy Hollow Presbyterian Church, Presbyterian, San Anselmo

South Berkeley Community Church, United Church of Christ, Berkeley

St. Augustine's Episcopal Church, Episcopal, Oakland

St. Gregory of Nyssa Episcopal Church, Episcopal, San Francisco

United Methodist Church of Daly City, United Methodist Church, Daly City

Valley Presbyterian Church, Presbyterian, Portola Valley

ORIGINAL MUSIC OR LITURGICAL TEXTS CREATED BY MUSIC STAFF OR MEMBERS OF THE CONGREGATION

Albany UMC, United Methodist Church, Albany

All Saints' Episcopal Church, Episcopal, Palo Alto

All Saints' Episcopal Church, Episcopal, San Francisco

Asbury UMC, United Methodist Church, Livermore

Beth Eden Baptist Church, Baptist, Oakland

Bethany UMC, United Methodist Church, San Francisco

Bethel Community Presbyterian Church, Presbyterian, San Leandro

Broadmoor Presbyterian Church, Presbyterian, Daly City

Christ Episcopal Church, Episcopal, Los Altos

Christ Lutheran Church, Lutheran, San Francisco

Christ Presbyterian Church, Presbyterian, San Leandro

Church of the Holy Innocents, Episcopal, Corte Madera

College Heights Church, United Church of Christ, San Mateo

Community Congregational Church of Belvedere-Tiburon,
    United Church of Christ, Tiburon

Congregational Church of Belmont, United Church of Christ, Belmont

Covenant Presbyterian Church, Presbyterian, Palo Alto

Covenant Presbyterian Church, Presbyterian, San Francisco

Episcopal Church of St. Mary the Virgin, Episcopal, San Francisco

First Baptist Church, Baptist, Oakland

First Christian Church, Disciples of Christ, San Mateo

First Congregational UCC, United Church of Christ, Oakland

First Presbyterian Church, Presbyterian, Milpitas

First Presbyterian Church, Presbyterian, Oakland

First Presbyterian Church, Presbyterian, San Leandro

First UMC, United Methodist Church, Campbell

First UMC, United Methodist Church, San Rafael

Good Shepherd Episcopal Church, Episcopal, Belmont

Grace Lutheran Church, Lutheran, Palo Alto

Hillsdale United Methodist, United Methodist Church, San Mateo

Holy Innocents' Episcopal Church, Episcopal, San Francisco

Los Gatos UMC, United Methodist Church, Los Gatos

Lutheran Church of Our Savior, Lutheran, San Francisco

Melrose UMC, United Methodist Church, Oakland

New Creation Lutheran Church, Lutheran, San Jose

New Life Church, Baptist, Richmond

New Spirit Community Church, United Church of Christ, Berkeley

Niles Congregational UCC, United Church of Christ, Fremont

Northminster Presbyterian Church, Presbyterian, El Cerrito

Ocean Avenue Presbyterian Church, Presbyterian, San Francisco

Plymouth UCC, United Church of Christ, Oakland

Presbyterian Church of Sunnyvale, Presbyterian, Sunnyvale

St. Aidan's Episcopal Church, Episcopal, San Francisco

St. Alban's Episcopal Church, Episcopal, Albany

St. Andrew's Episcopal Church, Episcopal, Saratoga

St. Columba Episcopal Church, Episcopal, Inverness

St. Francis of Assisi Episcopal Church, Episcopal, Novato

St. Francis' Episcopal Church, Episcopal, San Francisco

St. Gregory of Nyssa Episcopal Church, Episcopal, San Francisco

St. John-the-Evangelist Episcopal Church, Episcopal, San Francisco

St. Johns UCC, United Church of Christ, San Francisco

St. Joseph's Episcopal Church, Episcopal, Milpitas

St. Paul Lutheran Church, Lutheran, Oakland

St. Peter's Episcopal Church, Episcopal, San Francisco

St. Stephen's Episcopal Church, Episcopal, Belvedere

San Leandro Community Church, Baptist, San Leandro

San Martin Presbyterian Church, Presbyterian, San Martin

Seventh Avenue Presbyterian Church, Presbyterian, San Francisco

Skyline Community UCC, United Church of Christ, Oakland

Sleepy Hollow Presbyterian Church, Presbyterian, San Anselmo

Trinity Lutheran Church, Lutheran, Alameda

Trinity Lutheran Church, Lutheran, Oakland

Trinity UMC, United Methodist Church, Berkeley

University Lutheran Chapel, Lutheran, Berkeley

Valley Presbyterian Church, Presbyterian, Portola Valley

OTHER CREATIVE OR UNUSUAL ELEMENTS USED REGULARLY IN WORSHIP SERVICES

Bethel Presbyterian Church, Presbyterian, San Leandro

Broadmoor Presbyterian Church, Presbyterian, Daly City

College Heights Church, United Church of Christ, San Mateo

Congregational Church of Belmont , United Church of Christ, Belmont

Eden United Church of Christ, United Church of Christ, Hayward

First Congregational UCC, United Church of Christ, Alameda

First Presbyterian Church, Presbyterian, Milpitas

First United Methodist Church, United Methodist Church, San Rafael

Grace United Methodist Church of Saratoga, United Methodist Church, Saratoga

Holy Redeemer Lutheran Church , Lutheran, San Jose

New Spirit Community Church, United Church of Christ, Berkeley

Plymouth United Church of Christ, United Church of Christ, Oakland

Redwoods Presbyterian Church, Presbyterian, Larkspur

St. Gregory of Nyssa Episcopal Church, Episcopal, San Francisco

Sunset Ministry, Baptist, San Francisco

Valley Presbyterian church, Presbyterian, Portola Valley

AFFILIATED WITH CENTER FOR PROGRESSIVE CHRISTIANITY

College Heights Church, United Church of Christ, San Mateo

Fairfax Community Church, United Church of Christ, Fairfax

First Congregational UCC Church, United Church of Christ, Alameda

Good Shepherd Episcopal Church, Episcopal, Berkeley

Metropolitan Community Church of Greater Hayward, MCC, San Lorenzo

Metropolitan Community Church of San Jose, MCC, San Jose

Noe Valley Ministry, Presbyterian, San Francisco

St. John the Evangelist, Episcopal, San Francisco

Sausalito Presbyterian Church, Presbyterian, Sausalito

UNOFFICIAL DRESS CODE IS "PLAY CLOTHES" CASUAL

Bethany UMC, United Methodist Church, San Francisco

Christ Presbyterian Church, Presbyterian, San Leandro

Church of the Advent of Christ the King, Episcopal, San Francisco

Congregational Church of Belmont, United Church of Christ, Belmont

Holy Innocents' Episcopal Church, Episcopal, San Francisco

Lutheran Church of Our Savior, Lutheran, San Francisco

Morgan Hill United Methodist, United Methodist Church, Morgan Hill

St. Aidan's Episcopal Church, Episcopal, Bolinas

St. Aidan's Episcopal Church, Episcopal, San Francisco

St. Andrew Presbyterian Church, Presbyterian, Pacifica

St. James' Episcopal Church, Episcopal, San Francisco

Seventh Avenue Presbyterian Church, Presbyterian, San Francisco

Twenty-First Avenue Baptist Church, Baptist, San Francisco

SAME-SEX BLESSINGS

All Saints' Episcopal Church, Episcopal, Palo Alto

All Saints' Episcopal Church, Episcopal, San Francisco

Alum Rock UMC, United Methodist Church, San Jose

Broadmoor Presbyterian Church, Presbyterian, Daly City

Calvary Presbyterian Church, Presbyterian, San Francisco

Chalice Christian Church, Disciples of Christ, San Mateo

Christ Episcopal Church, Episcopal, Alameda

Christ Episcopal Church, Episcopal, Los Altos

Christ Lutheran Church, Lutheran, San Francisco

Christ Presbyterian Church in Terra Linda, Presbyterian, San Rafael

Christ the Victor Lutheran Church, Lutheran, Fairfax

Church of the Advent of Christ the King, Episcopal, San Francisco

College Heights Church, United Church of Christ, San Mateo

Community Church of Mill Valley, United Church of Christ, Mill Valley

Community Congregational Church of Belvedere-Tiburon,
    United Church of Christ, Tiburon

Congregational Church of Belmont, United Church of Christ, Belmont

Congregational Church of San Mateo, United Church of Christ, San Mateo

Covenant Presbyterian Church, Presbyterian, San Francisco

Episcopal Church of the Incarnation, Episcopal, San Francisco

Fairfax Community Church, United Church of Christ, Fairfax

Faith Lutheran Church, Lutheran, San Rafael

First Christian Church, Disciples of Christ, San Mateo

First Congregational Church, United Church of Christ, Berkeley

First Congregational UCC, United Church of Christ, Alameda

First Congregational UCC, United Church of Christ, Oakland

First Congregational UCC, United Church of Christ, San Jose

First Presbyterian Church of Palo Alto, Presbyterian, Palo AltoFirst UMC,
    United Methodist Church, San Rafael

Fremont Congregational UCC, United Church of Christ, Fremont

Good Shepherd Episcopal Church, Episcopal, Belmont

Holy Cross Episcopal Church, Episcopal, Castro Valley

Holy Innocents' Episcopal Church, Episcopal, San Francisco

Holy Redeemer Lutheran Church, Lutheran, San Jose

Immanuel Lutheran Church, Lutheran, San Jose

Ladera Community UCC, United Church of Christ, Portola Valley

Lake Merritt UMC, United Methodist Church, Oakland

Lutheran Church of Our Savior, Lutheran, San Francisco

Messiah Lutheran Church, Lutheran, Redwood City

Morgan Hill United Methodist, United Methodist Church, Morgan Hill

Niles Congregational UCC, United Church of Christ, Fremont

Noe Valley Ministry, Presbyterian, San Francisco

Northminster Presbyterian Church, Presbyterian, El Cerrito

Ocean Avenue Presbyterian Church, Presbyterian, San Francisco

Peace Lutheran Church, Lutheran, San Bruno

Plymouth UCC, United Church of Christ, Oakland

Redeemer Lutheran Church, Lutheran, Cupertino

Redwoods Presbyterian Church, Presbyterian, Larkspur

Resurrection Lutheran Church, Lutheran, Oakland

St. Aidan's Episcopal Church, Episcopal, Bolinas

St. Aidan's Episcopal Church, Episcopal, San Francisco

St. Andrew's Episcopal Church, Episcopal, Saratoga

St. Clare's Episcopal Church, Episcopal, Pleasanton

St. Edmund's Episcopal Church, Episcopal, Pacifica

St. Francis' Episcopal Church, Episcopal, San Francisco

St. Gregory of Nyssa Episcopal Church, Episcopal, San Francisco

St. James' Episcopal Church, Episcopal, San Francisco

St. John-the-Evangelist Episcopal Church, Episcopal, San Francisco

St. Johns UCC, United Church of Christ, San Francisco

St. Joseph's Episcopal Church, Episcopal, Milpitas

St. Jude's Episcopal Church, Episcopal, Cupertino

St. Luke's Episcopal Church, Episcopal, Los Gatos

St. Mark's Episcopal Church, Episcopal, Berkeley

St. Mark's Episcopal Church, Episcopal, Palo Alto

St. Paul Lutheran Church, Lutheran, Oakland

St. Peter's Episcopal Church, Episcopal, Redwood City

St. Peter's Episcopal Church, Episcopal, San Francisco

St. Stephen's Episcopal Church, Episcopal, Belvedere

St. Thomas' Episcopal Church, Episcopal, Sunnyvale

San Leandro Community Church, Baptist, San Leandro

San Lorenzo Community Church, United Church of Christ, San Lorenzo

Seventh Avenue Presbyterian Church, Presbyterian, San Francisco

Skyline Community UCC, United Church of Christ, Oakland

Trinity Episcopal Church, Episcopal, San Francisco

Trinity Lutheran Church, Lutheran, Oakland

Trinity UMC, United Methodist Church, Berkeley

University Lutheran Chapel, Lutheran, Berkeley

PARISH MISSION STATEMENT INCLUDES THE WORDS "INCLUSIVE" OR "WELCOMING"

Albany UMC, United Methodist Church, Albany

All Saints' Episcopal Church, Episcopal, Palo Alto

All Saints' Episcopal Church, Episcopal, San Francisco

Alum Rock UMC, United Methodist Church, San Jose

Bethany UMC, United Methodist Church, San Francisco

Chalice Christian Church, Disciples of Christ, San Mateo

Christ Episcopal Church, Episcopal, Los Altos

Christ the Good Shepherd Lutheran Church, Lutheran, San Jose

Christ the King Lutheran Church, Lutheran, Fremont

Christ Lutheran Church, Lutheran, San Francisco

College Heights Church, United Church of Christ, San Mateo

Community Congregational Church of Belvedere-Tiburon,
    United Church of Christ, Tiburon

Congregational Church of Belmont, United Church of Christ, Belmont

Congregational Church of San Mateo, United Church of Christ, San Mateo

Covenant Presbyterian Church, Presbyterian, San Francisco

Eden UCC, United Church of Christ, Hayward

Episcopal Church of the Incarnation, Episcopal, San Francisco

Episcopal Church of St. Mary the Virgin, Episcopal, San Francisco

Fairfax Community Church, United Church of Christ, Fairfax

First Christian Church, Disciples of Christ, San Mateo

First Congregational Church, United Church of Christ, Berkeley

First Congregational UCC, United Church of Christ, Alameda

First Congregational UCC, United Church of Christ, Oakland

First Congregational UCC, United Church of Christ, San Jose

First UMC, United Methodist Church, Campbell

First UMC, United Methodist Church, San Rafael

Fremont Congregational UCC, United Church of Christ, Fremont

Grace Lutheran Church, Lutheran, Palo Alto

Grace UMC of Saratoga, United Methodist Church, Saratoga

Hillsdale United Methodist, United Methodist Church, San Mateo

Hope Lutheran Church, Lutheran, El Sobrante

Immanuel Lutheran Church, Lutheran, San Jose

Ladera Community UCC, United Church of Christ, Portola Valley

Los Gatos UMC, United Methodist Church, Los Gatos

Lutheran Church of Our Savior, Lutheran, San Francisco

Marin Lutheran Church, Lutheran, Corte Madera

Melrose UMC, United Methodist Church, Oakland

Morgan Hill United Methodist, United Methodist Church, Morgan Hill

New Creation Lutheran Church, Lutheran, San Jose

Niles Congregational UCC, United Church of Christ, Fremont

Noe Valley Ministry, Presbyterian, San Francisco

Peace Lutheran Church, Lutheran, San Bruno

Plymouth UCC, United Church of Christ, Oakland

St. Aidan's Episcopal Church, Episcopal, Bolinas

St. Aidan's Episcopal Church, Episcopal, San Francisco

St. Ambrose Episcopal Church, Episcopal, Foster City

St. Andrew Presbyterian Church, Presbyterian, Pacifica

St. Andrew's Episcopal Church, Episcopal, San Bruno

St. Andrew's Episcopal Church, Episcopal, Saratoga

St. Edmund's Episcopal Church, Episcopal, Pacifica

St. Elizabeth's Episcopal Church, Episcopal, South San Francisco

St. Francis' Episcopal Church, Episcopal, San Francisco

St. Gregory of Nyssa Episcopal Church, Episcopal, San Francisco

St. James' Episcopal Church, Episcopal, Fremont

St. Johns UCC, United Church of Christ, San Francisco

St. Joseph's Episcopal Church, Episcopal, Milpitas

St. Jude's Episcopal Church, Episcopal, Cupertino

St. Luke's Episcopal Church, Episcopal, Los Gatos

St. Mark's Episcopal Church, Episcopal, Berkeley

St. Mark's Episcopal Church, Episcopal, Palo Alto

St. Paul Lutheran Church, Lutheran, Oakland

St. Paul's UMC, United Methodist Church, San Jose

St. Peter's Episcopal Church, Episcopal, Redwood City

St. Stephen's Episcopal Church, Episcopal, Belvedere

St. Stephens In-the-Field Episcopal Church, Episcopal, San Jose

St. Thomas' Episcopal Church, Episcopal, Sunnyvale

San Leandro Community Church, Baptist, San Leandro

Skyline Community UCC, United Church of Christ, Oakland

Sunnyhills UMC, United Methodist Church, Milpitas

Trinity Episcopal Church, Episcopal, San Francisco

Trinity Lutheran Church, Lutheran, Alameda

Trinity Lutheran Church, Lutheran, Oakland

Trinity UMC, United Methodist Church, Berkeley

United Methodist Church of Daly City, United Methodist Church, Daly City

University Lutheran Chapel, Lutheran, Berkeley

ALTERNATIVE SERVICES

Churches on this list offer alternatives to the traditional morning worship service, such as Taizé, Compline, quiet prayer, or contemplative prayer

Calvary Presbyterian Church, Presbyterian, San Francisco

College Heights Church, United Church of Christ, San Mateo

Community Church of Mill Valley, United Church of Christ, Mill Valley

Congregational Church of Belmont, United Church of Christ, Belmont

Congregational Church of San Mateo, United Church of Christ, San Mateo

Covenant Presbyterian Church, Presbyterian, Palo Alto

Faith Lutheran Church, Lutheran, San Rafael

First Christian Church, Disciples of Christ, Palo Alto

First Christian Church, Disciples of Christ, San Mateo

First Presbyterian Church, Presbyterian, Burlingame

First Presbyterian Church, Presbyterian, Milpitas

First UMC, United Methodist Church, Campbell

Good Shepherd Episcopal Church, Episcopal, Belmont

Holy Redeemer Lutheran Church, Lutheran, San Jose

Lutheran Church of Our Savior, Lutheran, San Francisco

Marin Lutheran Church, Lutheran, Corte Madera

New Spirit Community Church, United Church of Christ, Berkeley

Noe Valley Ministry, Presbyterian, San Francisco

Presbyterian Church of Sunnyvale, Presbyterian, Sunnyvale

Redwoods Presbyterian Church, Presbyterian, Larkspur

St. Aidan's Episcopal Church, Episcopal, San Francisco

St. Edmund's Episcopal Church, Episcopal, Pacifica

St. Elizabeth's Episcopal Church, Episcopal, South San Francisco

St. Gregory of Nyssa Episcopal Church, Episcopal, San Francisco

St. James' Episcopal Church, Episcopal, Fremont

St. Johns UCC, United Church of Christ, San Francisco

St. Paul's UMC, United Methodist Church, San Jose

St. Peter's Episcopal Church, Episcopal, Redwood City

St. Stephens In-the-Field Episcopal Church, Episcopal, San Jose

San Leandro Community Church, Baptist, San Leandro

Seventh Avenue Presbyterian Church, Presbyterian, San Francisco

South Berkeley Community Church, United Church of Christ, Berkeley

Sleepy Hollow Presbyterian Church, Presbyterian, San Anselmo

Church Listings

This section provides basic contact information for approximately four hundred individual congregations in the San Francisco Bay Area, sorted first by county (San Mateo, San Francisco, Santa Clara, Alameda, western Contra Costa, and Marin) and then by denomination (Episcopal, ELCA Lutheran, Presbyterian, United Methodist, United Church of Christ, American Baptist, Disciples of Christ). Within a denomination, the churches are listed in alphabetical order. Some of the information is from denominational web sites.

The seven denominations are the Big Five that together comprise what is generally considered mainline Protestantism—Baptists, Episcopalians, Lutherans, Methodists, and Presbyterians—plus two smaller denominations. I have included the United Church of Christ and the Disciples of Christ because they have lineages similar to the Big Five, traditions of independent thought, and a number of very interesting congregations in the Bay Area. Unitarians, Quakers, and Metropolitan Community Churches are not included in the listings below, (nor in the lists of churches sorted by attributes in the preceding section), but basic contact information is given for all of their Bay Area communities on page 187.

Some of the listings have only an address and phone number, while others have web site addresses and the times of Sunday morning services. To gather information beyond the basics, I mailed a questionnaire to each of the congregations listed, requesting that they respond in a very tight time period! Nearly half of the churches did, and their responses are the basis for the enhanced listings. Call for more information if there's a church that has caught your eye but has only basic information here. If you want to avoid speaking to a human, call at dinner time or late at night. Most churches have only part-time office hours, but nearly every one has an answering machine message that gives the times of the regular services.

Key for "dress code": In the questionnaire, churches were given the choice of describing what most people wear to services as "Sunday best" (SB); "casual Friday" (CF), meaning clothes that might be worn on dress-down day in a formal office; or "play clothes" (PC), meaning whatever people wear for the weekend.

A note on foreign language congregations and services: There are churches in all denominations that minister to culturally specific congregations in their native tongues. Since this is an English-language book, and the somewhat tight format of the listings doesn't allow for notation, I chose not to include those congregations here. A number of the churches on this list conduct services in other languages; and for the same set of reasons—mainly to reduce confusion—I haven't listed those services in this directory.

SAN MATEO COUNTY

EPISCOPAL

CHRIST EPISCOPAL CHURCH
815 Portola Road
Portola Valley, CA 94028-7206
Phone: 650.851.0224

EPISCOPAL CHURCH OF THE
EPIPHANY
1839 Arroyo Avenue
San Carlos, CA 94070-3899
Phone: 650.591.0328
E-mail: Epiph@aol.com

GOOD SHEPHERD EPISCOPAL
CHURCH
1300 Fifth Avenue
Belmont, CA 94002-3831
Phone: 650.593.4844
Sunday services: 8AM and 10AM
Dress code: CF

HOLY CHILD & SAINT MARTIN'S
EPISCOPAL CHURCH
777 Southgate Avenue
Daly City, CA 94015-3665
Phone: 650.991.1560

HOLY FAMILY EPISCOPAL CHURCH
1590 S Cabrillo Highway
Half Moon Bay, CA 94019-2245
Phone: 650.726.0506

SAINT AMBROSE EPISCOPAL
CHURCH
900 Edgewater Boulevard
Foster City, CA 94404-3709
Phone: 650.574.1369
Sunday services: 8AM and 10AM
Dress code: CF

SAINT ANDREW'S EPISCOPAL
CHURCH
1600 Santa Lucia Avenue
San Bruno, CA 94066-4798
Phone: 650.583.6678
E-mail: standrewsanbruno@juno.com
Web site: www.StAndrewepiscopal.org
Sunday service: 10AM
Dress code: CF

SAINT BEDE'S EPISCOPAL CHURCH
2650 Sand Hill Road
Menlo Park, CA 94025-7018
Phone: 650.854.6555

SAINT EDMUND'S EPISCOPAL
CHURCH
1500 Perez Drive
Pacifica, CA 94044-6611
Phone: 650.359-3364
Web site: www.saint-edmunds.org
Sunday services: 8AM and 10AM
Dress code: CF

SAINT ELIZABETH'S EPISCOPAL
CHURCH
280 Country Club Drive
South San Francisco, CA 94080-5743
Phone: 650.583.3720
Web site: www.stelizabeth.tripod.com
Sunday services: 8AM and 10AM
Dress code: CF

SAINT MATTHEW'S EPISCOPAL
CHURCH
1 S El Camino Real
San Mateo, CA 94401
Phone: 650.342.1481

SAINT PAUL'S EPISCOPAL CHURCH
415 El Camino Real
Burlingame, CA 94010-5197
Phone: 650.348.4811
E-mail: stpauls-burl@diocal.org

SAINT PETER'S EPISCOPAL
CHURCH
178 Clinton Street
Redwood City, CA 94062-1583
Phone: 650.367.0777
E-mail: office@stpetersrwc.org
Web site: www.stpersrwc.org
Sunday services: 8AM and 10AM
Dress code: CF

TRANSFIGURATION EPISCOPAL
CHURCH
3900 Alameda de las Pulgas
San Mateo, CA 94403-4110
Phone: 650.341.8206

TRINITY EPISCOPAL PARISH
330 Ravenswood Avenue
Menlo Park, CA 94025-3420
Phone: 650.326.2083
E-mail: office@trinitymenlopark.org

LUTHERAN

CALVARY LUTHERAN CHURCH
Santa Lucia & Cypress Avenue
Millbrae, CA 94030
Phone: 650.588.2840

COASTSIDE LUTHERAN CHURCH
900 N Cabrillo Highway
Half Moon Bay, CA 94019
Phone: 650.726.9293
E-mail: info@coastsideluthern.org
Web site: www.coastsidelutheran.org
Sunday service: 10AM
Dress code: CF

HOLY CROSS LUTHERAN CHURCH
1165 Seville Drive
Pacifica, CA 94044
Phone: 650.359.2710
E-mail: HTLCSanCarlos@aol.com
Sunday service: 10:15AM

HOLY TRINITY LUTHERAN
CHURCH
149 Manzanita Avenue
San Carlos, CA 94070
Phone: 650.593.0325
Web site: www.lutherhouse.
org/HTLC-SCCA
Sunday service: 10:15AM

MESSIAH LUTHERAN CHURCH
1835 Valota Road
Redwood City, CA 94061
Phone: 650.369.5201
E-mail: MessiahLuth@aol.com
Web site: www.messiahjubilee.org
Sunday service: 10AM
Dress code: CF

OUR REDEEMER LUTHERAN
CHURCH
609 Southwood Drive at
El Camino Real
South San Francisco, CA 94083-5568
Phone: 650.583.5622

PEACE LUTHERAN CHURCH
850 Glenview Drive
San Bruno, CA 94066
Phone: 650.589.6617
E-mail: peace_lutheran@netzero.com
Sunday service: 10:30AM
Dress code: CF

SAINT ANDREW'S LUTHERAN
CHURCH
1501 S El Camino Real
San Mateo, CA 94022
Phone: 650.345.1625
Web site: www.standrews-sanmateo.org
Sunday services: 8AM and 10:30AM

PRESBYTERIAN

BETHANY PRESBYTERIAN CHURCH
2400 Rosewood Drive
San Bruno, CA 94066
Phone: 650.589.3711

BROADMOOR PRESBYTERIAN
CHURCH
377 87th Street
Daly City, CA 94015
Phone: 650.755.0597
Sunday service: 10AM
Dress code: CF

FIRST PRESBYTERIAN CHURCH
1500 Easton Drive
Burlingame, CA 94010
Phone: 650.342.0875
E-mail: FPCB1@best.com
Web site: www.burlpres.org
Sunday services: 8:30AM, 9:30AM,
and 11AM
Dress code: SB

GRACE PRESBYTERIAN CHURCH
515 Winchester Street
Daly City, CA 94014
Phone: 415.586.5681

MENLO PARK PRESBYTERIAN
CHURCH
950 Santa Cruz Avenue
Menlo Park, CA 94025
Phone: 650.323.8600
Web site: www.mppc.org/
Services: Sunday 8AM, 9:30AM, and
11AM; Saturday 5AM

SAINT ANDREW PRESBYTERIAN
CHURCH
1125 Terra Nova Boulevard
Pacifica, CA 94044
Phone: 650.359.2462
Sunday service: 9:15AM
Dress code: PC

TRINITY PRESBYTERIAN CHURCH
1106 Alameda Pulgas
San Carlos, CA 94070
Phone: 650.593.8226
Web site: www.trinity-
pres.org/index2.html

VALLEY PRESBYTERIAN CHURCH
945 Portola Road
Portola Valley, CA 94028
Phone: 650.851.8282
E-mail: ornes@valleypreschurch.org
Web site: www.valleypreschurch.org/
Sunday services: 8:30AM and 10:30AM

METHODIST

ALDERSGATE UNITED METHODIST
CHURCH/SAINT PAUL'S UNITED
METHODIST CHURCH
500 Miller Avenue
South San Francisco, CA 94080
Phone: 650.583.6757

BURLINGAME UNITED METHODIST
CHURCH
1443 Howard Avenue
Burlingame, CA 94010
Phone: 650.344.6321

COMMUNITY UNITED METHODIST
CHURCH
777 Miramontes Street
Half Moon Bay, CA 94019
Phone: 650.726.4621
E-mail: cumc@coastside.net
Web site: www.cumc-hmb.com
Sunday services: 8AM, 9AM, and 11AM
Dress code: SB

CRYSTAL SPRINGS UNITED
METHODIST CHURCH
2145 Bunker Hill Drive
San Mateo, CA 94402
Phone: 650.345.2381

DALY CITY UNITED METHODIST
CHURCH
1474 Southgate Avenue
Daly City, CA 94015
Phone: 650.992.5530
Sunday service: 11AM
Dress code: SB

FIRST UNITED METHODIST
CHURCH
2915 Broadway
Redwood City, CA 94062
Phone: 650.366.0331

HILLSDALE UNITED METHODIST
CHURCH
303 W 36th Avenue
San Mateo, CA 94403
Phone: 650.345.8514
Sunday services: 8:30AM and 10:30AM
Dress code: CF

MILLBRAE UNITED METHODIST
CHURCH
450 Chadbourne Avenue
Millbrae, CA 94030
Phone: 650.697.8300

SAN BRUNO UNITED METHODIST
CHURCH
560 El Camino Real
San Bruno, CA 94066
Phone: 650.588.6372

SHOREVIEW UNITED METHODIST
CHURCH
120 Lindbergh Street
San Mateo, CA 94401
Phone: 650.344.7410

WOODSIDE ROAD UNITED
METHODIST CHURCH
2000 Woodside Road
Redwood City, CA 94061
Phone: 650.368.3376

UNITED CHURCH OF CHRIST

COLLEGE HEIGHTS UNITED
CHURCH OF CHRIST
1150 W Hillsdale Boulevard
San Mateo, CA 94403-3120
Phone: 650.341.7311
Web site: www.openchristianity.com
Sunday service: 10AM
Dress code: CF and PC

COMMUNITY UNITED CHURCH OF
CHRIST
1336 Arroyo Avenue
San Carlos, CA 94070-3998
Phone: 650.593.7809
E-mail: uccsc@netwiz.net
Web site: www.uccsc.org
Sunday service: 10AM

CONGREGATIONAL CHURCH OF
BELMONT
751 Alameda de las Pulgas
Belmont, CA 94002-1606
Phone: 650.593.4547
E-mail: BelmontUCC@aol.com
Web site: www.uccbelmont.org
Sunday service: 10:30AM
Dress code: PC

CONGREGATIONAL UNITED
CHURCH OF CHRIST
225 Tilton Avenue
San Mateo, CA 94401-2825
Phone: 650.343.3694
E-mail: ccsm@pacbell.net
Web site: www.ccsm-ucc.org
Sunday service: 10:30AM
Dress code: SB and CF

FIRST CONGREGATIONAL UNITED
CHURCH OF CHRIST
2323 Euclid Avenue
Redwood City, CA 94061-2099
Phone: 650.369.0344
E-mail: fccrc@concentric.net
Web site: www.concentric.net/~Fccrc
Sunday services: 9:30AM and 11AM
(no 11AM service in summer)

ISLAND UNITED CHURCH
1130 Balclutha Drive
Foster City, CA 94404-1710
Phone: 650.349.3544

LADERA COMMUNITY UNITED
CHURCH OF CHRIST
3300 Alpine Road
Portola Valley, CA 94028-7525
Phone: 650.854.5481
E-mail: church@ladera.org
Web site: www.ladera.org
Sunday service: 9:30AM

SAINT JOHNS UNITED CHURCH
OF CHRIST
480 San Anselmo Avenue N
San Bruno, CA 94066-0944
Phone: 650.588.4972

VILLAGE UNITED CHURCH OF
CHRIST
3154 Woodside Road
Woodside, CA 94062-2553
Phone: 650.851.1587
E-mail: wvc@natures-fx.org

BAPTIST

COMMUNITY BAPTIST CHURCH
15 S Humboldt Street
San Mateo, CA 94401
Phone: 650.342.0959

FIRST BAPTIST CHURCH
1430 Palm Drive
Burlingame, CA 94010
Phone: 650.579.5528

FIRST BAPTIST CHURCH
1100 Middle Avenue
Menlo Park, CA 94025
Phone: 650.323.8544

FIRST BAPTIST CHURCH
1005 Crystal Springs
San Bruno, CA 94066
Phone: 650.583.2871

FIRST BAPTIST CHURCH
787 Walnut Street
San Carlos, CA 94070
Phone: 650.593.8001

FIRST BAPTIST CHURCH
2801 Alameda de las Pulgas
San Mateo, CA 94403
Phone: 650.345.1965

MACEDONIA BAPTIST CHURCH
1110 Berkeley Avenue
Menlo Park, CA 94025
Phone: 650.325.0438

PILGRIM BAPTIST CHURCH
217 N Grant Street
San Mateo, CA 94401
Phone: 650.343.5415

TRINITY BAPTIST CHURCH
39 E 39th Avenue
San Mateo, CA 94403
Phone: 650.349.5311

VISTA DEL MAR BAPTIST CHURCH
1125 Terra Nova Boulevard
Pacifica, CA 94044
Phone: 650.355.6404

WESTLAKE COMMUNITY CHURCH
Southgate Avenue at Elmwood Avenue
Daly City, CA 94015
Phone: 650.756.5400
E-mail: Westlkbapt@aol.com

DISCIPLES OF CHRIST

CHALICE CHRISTIAN CHURCH
1164 Rickover Lane
Foster City, CA 94404
Phone: 650.358.9533

FIRST CHRISTIAN CHURCH
San Mateo, CA 94403
Services held in Buckham Room of
the Congregational Church of San
Mateo, 225 Tilton Avenue
Phone: 650.345.3137
Sunday services: 10:30AM
Dress code: FC

SAN FRANCISCO

EPISCOPAL

ALL SAINTS'
1350 Waller Street
San Francisco, CA 94117-2986
Phone: 415.621.1862
Web site: www.webmen.com/asp.htm
Sunday services: 8AM and 10AM

CHRIST EPISCOPAL CHURCH
2140 Pierce Street
San Francisco, 94115-2214
Phone: 415.921.6395

CHURCH OF THE ADVENT OF
CHRIST THE KING
261 Fell Street
San Francisco, CA 94102-5908
Phone: 415.431.0454
E-mail: adventusSF@aol.com
Sunday services: 8:30AM and 11AM
Dress code: PC

EPISCOPAL CHURCH OF THE
INCARNATION
1750 29th Avenue
San Francisco, CA 94122-4222
Phone: 415.564.2324
E-mail: comebefed@aol.com
Sunday services: 8AM and 10AM
Dress code: CF

EPISCOPAL CHURCH OF SAINT
MARY THE VIRGIN
2325 Union Street
San Francisco, CA 94123-3905
Phone: 415.921.3665
E-mail: office@smvsf.org
Web site: www.smvsf.org
Sunday services: 8AM, 9AM, 11AM,
5:30PM
Dress code: SB

HOLY INNOCENTS'
455 Fair Oaks Street
San Francisco, CA 94110-3618
Phone: 415.824.5142
E-mail: vicar@holyinsf.org
Web site: www.holyinsf.org
Sunday services: 9AM and 11AM
Dress code: PC

SAINT AIDAN'S EPISCOPAL
CHURCH
101 Gold Mine Drive
San Francisco, CA 94131-0526
Phone: 415.285.9540
E-mail: saintAidan@aol.com
Web site: www.saintAidan.org
Sunday services: 8AM and 10:10AM
Dress code: PC

SAINT CYPRIAN'S EPISCOPAL
CHURCH
2097 Turk Street
San Francisco, CA 94115-4326
Phone: 415.567.1855

SAINT FRANCIS' EPISCOPAL
CHURCH
399 San Fernando Way
San Francisco, CA 94127-1913
Phone: 415.334.1590
E-mail: stfrancis@stfrancisepiscopal.org
Web site: www.stfrancisepiscopal.org
Sunday services: 8AM and 10AM
Dress code: CF

SAINT GREGORY OF NYSSA
EPISCOPAL CHURCH
500 DeHaro Street
San Francisco, CA 94107-2306
Phone: 415.255.8100
E-mail: office@saintgregorys.org
Web site: www.saintgregorys.org
Sunday services: 8AM and 10AM
Dress code: CF

SAINT JAMES' EPISCOPAL CHURCH
4620 California Street
San Francisco, CA 94118-1299
Phone: 415.751.1198
E-mail: StJames@StJamesSF.org
Web site: www.StJamesSF.org
Sunday services: 8AM and 10AM
Dress code: PC

SAINT JOHN-THE-EVANGELIST
EPISCOPAL CHURCH
1661 15th Street
San Francisco, CA 94103
Phone: 415.861.1436
E-mail: stjohnsf@pacbell.net
Web site: home.pacbell.net/stjohnsf/
Sunday service: 11AM
Dress code: CF

SAINT LUKE'S EPISCOPAL CHURCH
1755 Clay Street
San Francisco, CA 94109-3682
Phone: 415.673.7327

SAINT PETER'S EPISCOPAL
CHURCH
420 29th Avenue
San Francisco, CA 94121
Phone: 415.751.4942
Web site: www.stpeters-sf.org
Sunday services: 8AM and 10AM
Dress code: CF

TRINITY EPISCOPAL CHURCH
1668 Bush Street
San Francisco, CA 94109
Phone: 415.775.1117
E-mail: trinitysf@earthlink.net
Sunday services: 8AM and 11AM
Dress code: CF

LUTHERAN

CHRIST LUTHERAN CHURCH
1090 Quintara Street
San Francisco, CA 94116
Phone: 415.664.0915
Web site: www.unidial.
   com~christchurch
Sunday service: 10AM
Dress code: CF

EBENEZER LUTHERAN CHURCH
678 Portola Drive
San Francisco, CA 94127
Phone: 415.681.5400

GOLDEN GATE LUTHERAN
CHURCH
601 Dolores Street
San Francisco, CA 94110
Phone: 415.647.5050
Web site: www.GGLC.lutheran.com
Sunday service: 11AM

GRACE LUTHERAN CHURCH
3201 Ulloa Street
San Francisco, CA 94116
Phone: 415.731.1305

LUTHERAN CHURCH OF
OUR SAVIOR
1011 Garfield Street
San Francisco, CA 94132
Phone: 415.586.7890
Sunday service: 9:30AM
Dress code: PC

SAINT MARK'S LUTHERAN
CHURCH
1101 O'Farrell Street
San Francisco, CA 94109-6601
Phone: 415.928.7770
Web site: www.stmarks-sf.org
Sunday services: 9AM and 11AM

SAINT MARY AND SAINT MARTHA
LUTHERAN CHURCH
1050 S Van Ness Avenue
San Francisco, CA 94110-2616
Phone: 415.647.2717

SAINT MATTHEW LUTHERAN
CHURCH
3281 16th Street
San Francisco, CA 94103
Phone: 415.863.6371

SAINT PAULUS LUTHERAN
CHURCH
930 Gough Street
San Francisco, CA 94102
Phone: 415.673.8088

PRESBYTERIAN

CALVARY PRESBYTERIAN CHURCH
2515 Fillmore Street
San Francisco, CA 94115
Phone: 415.346.3832
Web site: www.calvarypresbyterian.
 org/
Sunday services: 8:45AM, 10AM, and
 11AM
Dress code: SB

CHINATOWN PRESBYTERIAN
CHURCH
925 Stockton Street
San Francisco, CA 94108
Phone: 415.392.1500

CHRIST PRESBYTERIAN CHURCH
1700 Sutter Street
San Francisco, CA 94115
Phone: 415.567.3988

COVENANT PRESBYTERIAN
CHURCH
321 Taraval Street
San Francisco, CA 94116
Phone: 415.664.5335
Sunday service: 10:30AM
Dress code: CF

FIRST UNITED PRESBYTERIAN
CHURCH
1740 Sloat Boulevard
San Francisco, CA 94132
Phone: 415.681.5780

INGLESIDE PRESBYTERIAN
CHURCH
1345 Ocean Avenue
San Francisco, CA 94112
Phone: 415.587.4472
Sunday service: 10:30AM
Dress code: SB

LAKESIDE PRESBYTERIAN CHURCH
201 Eucalyptus Drive
San Francisco, CA 94132
Phone: 415.564.8833
Web site: members.aol.com
 /lakesidechurch
Sunday service: 11AM (10AM
 in summer)

LINCOLN PARK PRESBYTERIAN
CHURCH
417 31st Avenue
San Francisco, CA 94121
Phone: 415.751.1140
Sunday service: 10AM

NEW LIBERATION PRESBYTERIAN
CHURCH
1100 Divisadero Street
San Francisco, CA 94115
Phone: 415.929.8881

NOE VALLEY MINISTRY
PRESBYTERIAN CHURCH
1021 Sanchez Street
San Francisco, CA 94114
Phone: 415.282.2317
Web site: www.noevalleyministry.org
Sunday service: 10:30AM
Dress code: CF

OCEAN AVENUE PRESBYTERIAN
CHURCH
32 Ocean Avenue
San Francisco, CA 94112
Phone: 415.587.1100
E-mail: oceanavepc@aol.com
Sunday service: 10AM
Dress code: CF

OLD FIRST PRESBYTERIAN
CHURCH
1751 Sacramento Street
San Francisco, CA 94109
Phone: 415.776.5552
Web site: www.oldfirst.org/
Sunday service: 11AM

SAINT JAMES PRESBYTERIAN
CHURCH
240 Leland Avenue
San Francisco, CA 94134
Phone: 415.586.6381

SAINT JOHNS PRESBYTERIAN
CHURCH
25 Lake Street
San Francisco, CA 94118
Phone: 415.751.1626

SAINT PAUL'S PRESBYTERIAN
CHURCH
1399 43rd Avenue
San Francisco, CA 94122
Phone: 415.566.7838
Sunday service: 11AM
Dress code: CF

SEVENTH AVENUE PRESBYTERIAN
CHURCH
1329 Seventh Avenue
San Francisco, CA 94122
Phone: 415.664.2543
E-mail: sapc@sdiworld.org
Web site: www.7thavechurch.com or
   www.sapcsf.org
Sunday service: 10AM
Dress code: PC

METHODIST

BETHANY UNITED METHODIST
CHURCH
1268 Sanchez Street
San Francisco, CA 94114
Phone: 415.647.8393
E-mail: BethanyUMC@aol.co
Web site: www.Bethanysf.org
Sunday services: 11AM (10AM
   in summer)
Dress code: PC

CALVARY UNITED METHODIST
CHURCH
1400 Judah Street
San Francisco, CA 94122
Phone: 415.566.3704

CENTRAL UNITED METHODIST
CHURCH
750 14th Street
San Francisco, CA 94114
Phone: 415.586.0383

FIRST SAINT JOHN'S UNITED
METHODIST CHURCH
1600 Clay Street
San Francisco, CA 94109
Phone: 415.474.6219

GENEVA AVENUE UNITED
METHODIST CHURCH
1261 Geneva Avenue
San Francisco, CA 94112
Phone: 415.585.6263

GLIDE MEMORIAL UNITED
METHODIST CHURCH
330 Ellis Street
San Francisco, CA 94102
Phone: 415.771.6300

GRACE UNITED METHODIST
CHURCH
2540 Taraval Street
San Francisco, CA 94116
Phone: 415.731.3050

HAMILTON UNITED METHODIST
CHURCH
1525 Waller Street
San Francisco, CA 94117
Phone: 415.566.2416

JONES MEMORIAL UNITED
METHODIST CHURCH
1975 Post Street
San Francisco, CA 94115
Phone: 415.921.7653

PARK PRESIDIO UNITED
METHODIST CHURCH
4301 Geary Boulevard
San Francisco, CA 94118
Phone: 415.751.4438

PINE UNITED METHODIST
CHURCH
426 33rd Avenue
San Francisco, CA 94121
Phone: 415.387.1800

RIDGE VIEW UNITED METHODIST
CHURCH
590 Leland Avenue
San Francisco, CA 94131
Phone: 415.239.5457

UNITED CHURCH OF CHRIST

CITY OF REFUGE COMMUNITY
1025 Howard Street
San Francisco, CA 94103
Phone: 415.861.6130
Web site: www.sfrefuge.org
Sunday service: 1PM

FIRST CONGREGATIONAL UNITED
CHURCH OF CHRIST
432 Mason Street
San Francisco, CA 94102-1799
Phone: 415.392.7461
E-mail: office@sanfranciscoucc.org
Web site: www.sanfranciscoucc.org
Sunday service: 11AM

PILGRIM COMMUNITY UNITED
CHURCH OF CHRIST
400 Randolph Street
San Francisco, CA 94132
Phone: 415.586.3124

SAINT JOHNS UNITED CHURCH OF
CHRIST
501 Laguna Honda Boulevard
San Francisco, CA 94127-1094
Phone: 415.731.9333
E-mail: office@stjohnsucc.org
Web site: www.sfstjohnsucc.org/
Sunday service: 10AM
Dress code: CF

BAPTIST

COMMUNITY BAPTIST CHURCH
1642 Broderick Street
San Francisco, CA 94115
Phone: 415.567.3248

COSMOPOLITAN BAPTIST CHURCH
199 Farallones Street
San Francisco, CA 94112
Phone: 415.584.7776

DOUBLE ROCK BAPTIST CHURCH
1591 Shafter Street
San Francisco, CA 94124
Phone: 415.822.6979

FIRST BAPTIST CHURCH
21 Octavia Street
San Francisco, CA 94102
Phone: 415.863.3382
Web site: www.fbcsf.org
Sunday services: 10:45AM and 7PM
Dress code: CF

GRACE BAPTIST CHURCH
PO Box 24417
San Francisco, CA 94124
Phone: 415.282.9622

HILLSIDE BAPTIST CHURCH
904 Rhode Island
San Francisco, CA 94107
Phone: 415.285.9094

PORTOLA BAPTIST CHURCH
25 Pioche Street
San Francisco, CA 94124
Phone: 415.584.3230

SAINT JAMES BAPTIST CHURCH
1470 Hudson Avenue
San Francisco, CA 94124
Phone: 415.648.5995

SAINT PAUL'S TABERNACLE
14 Vidal Drive
San Francisco, CA 94132
Phone: 415.469.5694

SUNSET MINISTRY
3010 Noriega Street
San Francisco, CA 94122
Phone: 415.753.3950
E-mail: office@sunsetministry.com
Web site: www.sunsetministry.org
Sunday services: 9AM and 11AM
Dress code: PC

TEMPLE BAPTIST CHURCH
3355 19th Avenue
San Francisco, CA 94132
Phone: 415.566.4080

THIRD BAPTIST CHURCH
1399 McAllister Street
San Francisco, CA 94115
Phone: 415.346.4426

TWENTY-FIRST AVENUE BAPTIST
CHURCH
380 21st Avenue
San Francisco, CA 94121
Phone: 415.751.9577
Sunday service: 11AM
Dress code: PC

DISCIPLES OF CHRIST

FIRST CHRISTIAN CHURCH
599 Duboce Avenue
San Francisco, CA 94117-3412
Phone: 415.621.9207

FOREST HILL CHRISTIAN CHURCH
250 Laguna Honda Boulevard
San Francisco, CA 94116
Phone: 415.566.1414
E-mail: foresthillcc@worldnet.att.net
Web site: www.forministry.com/church
/home.asp?SiteID=94116FHC
Sunday service: 10:45AM

SANTA CLARA COUNTY

EPISCOPAL

ALL SAINTS'
555 Waverley Street
Palo Alto, CA 94301
Phone: 650.322.4552
E-mail: info@asaints.org
Web site: www.asaints.org
Sunday services: 8AM and 10:30AM
Dress code: CF

CHRIST EPISCOPAL CHURCH
1040 Border Road
Los Altos, CA 94024-4725
Phone: 650.948.2151
Sunday services: 8AM, 9:15AM, and
10:15AM

CHURCH OF THE HOLY SPIRIT
65 W Rincon Road
Campbell, CA 95008
Phone: 408.374.4440
E-mail: hsec@earthlink.net

EPISCOPAL CHURCH IN THE
ALMADEN
6581 Camden Avenue
San Jose, CA 95120
Phone: 408.268.0243

HOLY CHILD EPISCOPAL CHURCH
2650 Aborn Road
San Jose, CA 95121

SAINT ANDREW'S EPISCOPAL
CHURCH
13601 Saratoga Avenue
Saratoga, CA 95070
Phone: 408.867.3493
E-mail: standrew@pacbell.net
Web site: www. st-andrews-saratoga.org
Sunday services: 8AM and 10AM
Dress code: CF

SAINT EDWARD'S
15040 Union Avenue
San Jose, CA 95124
Phone: 408.377.0129

SAINT FRANCIS'
1205 Pine Avenue
San Jose, CA 95125
Phone: 408.292.7090
E-mail:
stfran@stfrancisepiscopalchurch.org
Web site: www.stfrancisepiscopal
  church.org

SAINT JOHN THE DIVINE
11740 Peak Avenue
Morgan Hill, CA 95037
Phone: 408.779.9510
E-mail: stjohnmh@ibm.net

SAINT JOSEPH'S
355 Dixon Road
Milpitas, CA 95035
Phone: 408.262.4008
Web site: www.gomilpitas.com
  /episcopal/
Sunday services: 7:45AM and 10:30AM
Dress code: CF

SAINT JUDE'S
20929 McClellan Road
Cupertino, CA 95014
Phone: 408.252.4166
E-mail: saintjudes@aol.com
Web site: www.saintjudes.org
Sunday services: 8AM and 10:30AM
Dress code: CF

SAINT LUKE'S
20 University Avenue
Los Gatos, CA 95030
Phone: 408.354.2195
E-mail: stlukeslg@aol.com
Sunday services: 8AM, 9AM, and 11AM
Dress code: CF

SAINT MARK'S EPISCOPAL
CHURCH
600 Colorado Avenue
Palo Alto, CA 94306-2599
Phone: 650.326.3800
E-mail: stmarkse@pacbell.net
Sunday services: 8AM and 10AM
Dress code: CF

SAINT MARK'S
1957 Pruneridge Avenue
Santa Clara, CA 95050
Phone: 408.296.8383

SAINT PHILIP'S
5038 Hyland Avenue
San Jose, CA 95127
Phone: 408.251.8621
E-mail: stphilips@worldnet.att.net
Sunday services: 8AM and 10:30AM
Dress code: PC

SAINT STEPHEN'S
651 Broadway
Gilroy, CA 95020
Phone: 408.842.4413
E-mail: StGarlic@juno.com

SAINT STEPHEN'S IN THE FIELD
7629 Santa Teresa Boulevard
San Jose, CA 95139
Phone: 408.629.1836
E-mail: ststephenssj@bipgplanet.com
Sunday service: 10AM
Dress code: CF (mixed)

SAINT TIMOTHY'S
2094 Grant Road
Mountain View, CA 94040
Phone: 650.967.4724
E-mail: info@sttims.org
Web site: www.sttims.org
Sunday services: 8AM, 9:15AM,
10:45AM, and 5PM

LUTHERAN

ADVENT LUTHERAN CHURCH
16870 Murphy Avenue
Morgan Hill, CA 95037
Phone: 408.779-3551
Web site: www.garlic.com/~advent
Sunday services: 8AM and 10:45AM

ALL SAINTS LUTHERAN CHURCH
22445 Cupertino Avenue
Cupertino, CA 95041
Phone: 408.253.4300
Sunday service: 9:30AM

BETHEL LUTHERAN CHURCH
10181 Finch Avenue
Cupertino, CA 95014-4224
Phone: 408.252.8500
Web site: www.bethelcupertino.org
Sunday services: 8:45AM, 10AM,
and 11AM

**CHRIST THE GOOD SHEPHERD
LUTHERAN CHURCH**
1550 Meridian Avenue
San Jose, CA 95125
Phone: 408.266.8022
E-mail: CGSchurch@aol.com
Sunday service: 10AM
Dress code: CF

FAITH LUTHERAN CHURCH
16548 Ferris Avenue
Los Gatos, CA 95032
Phone: 408.356.5055
Web site: www.best.com
    /~faithlut/html/FaithHome.htm
Sunday services: 8AM and 10AM

**FIRST EVANGELICAL LUTHERAN
CHURCH**
600 Homer Avenue
Palo Alto, CA 94301
Phone: 650.322.4669
E-mail: luther@flcpa.org
Web site: www.flcpa.org
Sunday service: 10:30AM

GLORIA DEI LUTHERAN CHURCH
121 S White Road
San Jose, CA 95127
Phone: 408.729.7563
Sunday service: 9:30AM

GRACE LUTHERAN CHURCH
3149 Waverley Street
Palo Alto, CA 94306
Phone: 650.494.1212
E-mail: gluthernpaloalto.org
Sunday services: 8AM and 10:30AM
Dress code: CF

GRACE LUTHERAN CHURCH
2650 Aborn Road
San Jose, CA 95121
Phone: 408.274.1200
Web site: www.ihot.com/~gracelc
Sunday services: 8:15AM and 10:45AM

HOLY REDEEMER LUTHERAN
CHURCH
1948 The Alameda
San Jose, CA 95126
Phone: 408.296.4040
E-mail: HRLC95126@aol.com
Web site: www.scvlp.org
Sunday services: 8:45AM and 10AM
Dress code: CF

HOPE LUTHERAN CHURCH
600 W 42nd Avenue
San Mateo, CA 94403
Phone: 650.349.0100

HOPE LUTHERAN CHURCH
2383 Pacific Drive
Santa Clara, CA 95051-1415
Phone: 408.248.3668
E-mail: hopetoall@aol.com
Web site: members.aol.com/hopetoall
Sunday service: 9:30AM
Dress code: SB

IMMANUEL LUTHERAN CHURCH
1715 Grant Road
Los Altos, CA 94024
Phone: 650.967.4906
Web site: www.immanuel-losaltos.org/
Sunday services: 8AM, 9:15AM, and
10:45AM

IMMANUEL LUTHERAN CHURCH
1710 Moorpark Avenue
San Jose, CA 95128
Phone: 408.297.0993
Web site: www.scvlp.org
Sunday services: 8:15AM and 10AM
Dress code: CF

LOS ALTOS LUTHERAN CHURCH
460 S El Monte Avenue
Los Altos, CA 94022
Phone: 650.948.3012
Sunday services: 8:30AM and 10:45AM

NEW CREATION LUTHERAN
CHURCH
7275 Santa Teresa Boulevard
San Jose, CA 95139
Phone: 408.972.9200
E-mail: PastorK@pacbell.net
Web site: new.creation.tripod.com
Sunday service: 10:15AM
Dress code: CF

OUR SAVIOR'S LUTHERAN
CHURCH
1224 N Winchester Boulevard
Santa Clara, CA 95050
Phone: 408.296.2688
Sunday service: 10:15AM

REDEEMER LUTHERAN CHURCH
940 S Stelling Road
Cupertino, CA 95014
Phone: 408.253.5152
E-mail: rdmr@flash.net
Web site: www.flash.net/~rdmr/
Sunday service: 9:30AM
Dress code: CF

SAINT ANDREW LUTHERAN
CHURCH
5805 Cahalan Avenue
San Jose, CA 95123
Phone: 408.225.3565
E-mail:
StAndrewlutheran@NetZero.net

SAINT JOHN'S LUTHERAN
CHURCH
581 E Fremont Avenue
Sunnyvale, CA 94087
Phone: 408.739.2625
Web site: www.luther95.net
/SJLC-SCA
Sunday service: 11AM

SAINT LUKE LUTHERAN CHURCH
1025 The Dalles
Sunnyvale, CA 94087
Phone: 408.736.9216
Web site: stlukechurch.org/
Sunday service: 9AM

SAINT TIMOTHY LUTHERAN
CHURCH
5100 Camden Avenue
San Jose, CA 95124
Phone: 408.264.3858
Web site: www.st-tims-lutheran.org
Services: Sunday 8:30AM and 11AM,
Saturday 6PM

UNIVERSITY LUTHERAN CHURCH
1611 Stanford Avenue
Palo Alto, CA 94306
Phone:650.857.9660
Web site: www.stanford.edu
  /group/LSM/index.html
Sunday service: 10AM

PRESBYTERIAN

CALVIN PRESBYTERIAN CHURCH
890 Meridian Avenue
San Jose, CA 95126
Phone: 408.286.6633
E-mail: info@calvinchurch.org
Web site: www.calvinchurch.org/
Sunday service: 10AM

CHRIST PRESBYTERIAN CHURCH
5331 Dent Avenue
San Jose, CA 95118
Phone: 408.264.8966

COVENANT PRESBYTERIAN
CHURCH
670 E Meadow Drive
Palo Alto, CA 94306
Phone: 415.494.1760
Web site: www.covenant.palo-alto.ca.us
Sunday service: 10:45AM
Dress code: CF

EVERGREEN PRESBYTERIAN
CHURCH
San Jose, CA 95121
Services held at Evergreen
Community Center
4860 San Felipe Road, San Jose
Phone: 408.270-7700
Web site: www.evergreenchurch
  .netministries.org/
Sunday service: 9:30AM

FIRST PRESBYTERIAN CHURCH
1000 S Park Victoria Drive
Milpitas, CA 95035
Phone: 408.262.8000
E-mail: info@fpcm.org
Web site: www.fpcm.org
Sunday services: 9AM, 10:45AM,
  and 6:30PM
Dress code: CF

FIRST PRESBYTERIAN CHURCH
1667 Miramonte Avenue
Mountain View, CA 94040
Phone: 650.968.4473
E-mail: office@fpcmv.org
Web site: www.fpcmv.org
Sunday service: 10:30AM
Dress code: CF

FIRST PRESBYTERIAN CHURCH OF
PALO ALTO
1140 Cowper Street
Palo Alto, CA 94301
Phone: 650.325.5659
Web site: www.fprespa.org
Sunday service: 11AM (10AM in
  summer)
Dress code: CF

FIRST PRESBYTERIAN CHURCH
49 N Fourth Street
San Jose, CA 95112
Phone: 408.297.7212

FIRST PRESBYTERIAN CHURCH
2499 Homestead Road
Santa Clara, CA 95050
Phone: 408.984.0804
E-mail: fpcofsc@aol.com
Web site: www.fpcofsc.org/
Sunday service: 10AM
Dress code: CF

FOOTHILL PRESBYTERIAN CHURCH
5301 McKee Road
San Jose, CA 95127
Phone: 408.258.8133
E-mail: foothillpc@yahoo.com
Web site: www.foothillpc.org
Sunday service: 10:30AM

GILROY PRESBYTERIAN CHURCH
Gilroy, CA 95021
Phone: 408.842.3000

IMMANUEL PRESBYTERIAN CHURCH
3675 Payne Avenue
San Jose, CA 95117
Phone: 408.244.5298
E-mail: info@immanuel.org
Web site: www.immanuel.org
Sunday service: 9:30AM

MORGAN HILL PRESBYTERIAN
CHURCH
16970 Dewitt Avenue
Morgan Hill, CA 95037
Phone: 408.779.2820

PRESBYTERIAN CHURCH OF
LOS GATOS
16575 Shannon Road
Los Gatos, CA 95032
Phone: 408.356.6156
Web site: www.pclg.org/
Sunday service: 9:15AM
Dress code: CF

SAN MARTIN PRESBYTERIAN
CHURCH
13200 Lincoln Avenue
San Martin, CA 95046
Phone: 408.683.2908
Sunday service: 10:30AM
Dress code: CF

SANTA TERESA HILLS
PRESBYTERIAN CHURCH
5370 Snell Avenue
San Jose, CA 95123
Phone: 408.629.5906

SARATOGA PRESBYTERIAN
CHURCH
20455 Herriman Avenue
Saratoga, CA 95070
Phone: 408.867.0144
E-mail: spc@saratoga-ca.com
Web site: www.saratoga-ca
.com/spc.htm
Sunday service: 9:30AM

STONE CHURCH OF WILLOW GLEN
1108 Clark Way
San Jose, CA 95125
Phone: 408.269.1593
Web site: www.stonechurch.org
Sunday service: 9:30AM

PRESBYTERIAN CHURCH OF
SUNNYVALE
728 W Fremont Avenue
Sunnyvale, CA 94087
Phone: 408.739.1892
E-mail: info@svlpres.org
Web site: www.svlpres.org/
Sunday services: 9AM, 10:30AM,
and 5:45PM
Dress code: CF (morning),
PC (evening)

TRINITY PRESBYTERIAN CHURCH
3151 Union Avenue
San Jose, CA 95124
Phone: 408.377.8930
E-mail: trinpres@pacbell.net
Web site: www.trinitypresbyteriansj.org
Sunday service: 9:30AM
Dress code: SB

UNION PRESBYTERIAN CHURCH
858 University Avenue
Los Altos, CA 94024
Phone: 650.948.4361
Web site: www.unionpc.org/
Sunday service: 10:30AM

WESTHOPE PRESBYTERIAN
CHURCH
12850 Saratoga Avenue
Saratoga, CA 95070
Phone: 408.255.0955

WESTMINSTER PRESBYTERIAN
CHURCH
1100 Shasta Avenue
San Jose, CA 95126
Phone: 408.294.7447
Web site: www.westpres-sj.org
Sunday service: 10:30AM

WEST VALLEY PRESBYTERIAN
CHURCH
6191 Bollinger Road
Cupertino, CA 95014
Phone: 408.252.1365
Web site: www.wvpc.org
Sunday services: 9AM and 10:30AM
Dress code: SB

METHODIST

ALDERSGATE UNITED METHODIST
CHURCH
4243 Manuela Avenue
Palo Alto, CA 94306
Phone: 650.948.6806

ALMADEN HILLS UNITED
METHODIST CHURCH
1200 Blossom Hill Road
San Jose, CA 95118
Phone: 408.269.2345

ALUM ROCK UNITED METHODIST
CHURCH
30 Kirk Avenue
San Jose, CA 95127
Phone: 408.258.7368
Web site: gbgm-umc.org.alumrockumc
Sunday service: 10:30AM
Dress code: CF

CALVARY UNITED METHODIST
CHURCH
729 Morse Street
San Jose, CA 95126
Phone: 408.294.2204

CAMBRIAN PARK UNITED
METHODIST CHURCH
1919 Gunston Way
San Jose, CA 95124
Phone: 408.377.8155

EVERGREEN VALLEY UNITED
METHODIST CHURCH
3520 San Felipe Road
San Jose, CA 95135
Phone: 408.238.7631

FIRST UNITED METHODIST CHURCH
1675 S Winchester Boulevard
Campbell, CA 95008
Phone: 408.378.3472
E-mail: fumccampbell@juno.com
Sunday services: 9AM and 10:30AM
Dress code: CF

FIRST UNITED METHODIST CHURCH
625 Hamilton Avenue
Palo Alto, CA 94301
Phone: 650.323.6167

FIRST UNITED METHODIST CHURCH
24 N Fifth Street
San Jose, CA 95112
Phone: 408.294.7254

FIRST UNITED METHODIST CHURCH
535 Old San Francisco Road
Sunnyvale, CA 94086
Phone: 408.739.0826

GENESIS UNITED METHODIST
CHURCH
633 S Main Street
Milpitas, CA 95035
Phone: 408.263.9074

GILROY UNITED METHODIST
CHURCH
7600 Church Street
Gilroy, CA 95020
Phone: 408.842.4021

GOOD SAMARITAN UNITED
METHODIST CHURCH
19624 Homestead Road
Cupertino, CA 95014
Phone: 408.253.0751

GRACE UNITED METHODIST
CHURCH
19848 Prospect Road
Saratoga, CA 95070
Phone: 408.252.8268
Sunday service: 10AM
Dress code: varied

LOS ALTOS UNITED METHODIST
CHURCH
655 Magdalena Street
Los Altos, CA 94024
Phone: 415.948.1083

LOS GATOS UNITED METHODIST
CHURCH
19 High School Court
Los Gatos, CA 95032
Phone: 408.354.4730
*E-mail:*lgumc@kepnet.com
Web site: www.lgumc.org
Sunday services: 9:15AM and 11AM
Dress code: CF

MISSION CITY UNITED METHODIST
CHURCH
1700 Lincoln Street
Santa Clara, CA 95050
Phone: 408.345.9300

MORGAN HILL UNITED
METHODIST CHURCH
17175 Monterey
Morgan Hill, CA 95037
Phone: 408.779.4044
E-mail: mhumc@garlic.com
Web site: www.gbgm-
umc.org/ca_morganhill
Sunday services: 9:45AM
Dress code: PC

SAINT ANDREW'S UNITED
METHODIST CHURCH
4111 Alma Street
Palo Alto, CA 94306
Phone: 650.493.0900

SAINT PAUL'S UNITED METHODIST
CHURCH
405 S 10th Street
San Jose, CA 95112
Phone: 408.294.4564
Sunday service: 10:30AM
Dress code: CF

SUNNYHILLS UNITED METHODIST
CHURCH
355 Dixon Road
Milpitas, CA 95035
Phone: 408.262.1486
Sunday service: 9:30AM
Dress code: CF

TRINITY UNITED METHODIST
CHURCH
748 Mercy Street
Mountain View, CA 94041
Phone: 415.967.6283

TRINITY UNITED METHODIST
CHURCH
583 E Fremont Avenue
Sunnyvale, CA 94087
Phone: 408.739.1601

VALLEY FAITH UNITED
METHODIST CHURCH
1251 Sandia Avenue
Sunnyvale, CA 94089
Phone: 408.773.0177

WESLEY UNITED METHODIST
CHURCH
463 College Avenue
Palo Alto, CA 94306
Phone: 650.327.2092

WESLEY UNITED METHODIST
CHURCH
566 N Fifth Street
San Jose, CA 95112
Phone: 408.295.0367

WILLOW GLEN UNITED
METHODIST CHURCH
1420 Newport Avenue
San Jose, CA 95125
Phone: 408.294.9796

UNITED CHURCH OF CHRIST

ALMADEN VALLEY UNITED
CHURCH OF CHRIST
6581 Camden Avenue
San Jose, CA 95120-1908
Phone: 408.268.0243
Web site: www.avucc.org
Sunday service: 9AM
Dress code: CF

CHURCH OF THE VALLEY UNITED
CHURCH OF CHRIST
400 N Winchester Boulevard
Santa Clara, CA 95050-6397
Phone: 408.248.1050

CONGREGATIONAL CHURCH OF
CAMPBELL UNITED CHURCH OF
CHRIST
400 W Campbell Avenue
Campbell, CA 95008-1932
Phone: 408.378.4418

COSMOPOLITAN EVANGELICAL
UNITED CHURCH OF CHRIST
97 S Jackson Avenue
San Jose, CA 95116-2507
Phone: 408.272.8049

FIRST CONGREGATIONAL UNITED
CHURCH OF CHRIST
1980 Hamilton Avenue
San Jose, CA 95125-5686
Phone: 408.377.7121
E-mail: associate@firstccsj.org
Web site: www.firstccsj.org/
Sunday service: 10AM
Dress code: SB

FOOTHILLS CONGREGATIONAL
UNITED CHURCH OF CHRIST
461 Orange Avenue
Los Altos, CA 94022-3527
Phone: 650.948.8430
E-mail: F461Orange@aol.com
Web site: www.losaltosonline.com
/religion/FoothillsCC
Sunday services: 9AM and 10:30AM
(10AM only in summer)

NEW COMMUNITY OF FAITH
UNITED CHURCH OF CHRIST
6350 Rainbow Drive
San Jose, CA 95129-3999
Phone: 408.253.1408

SKYLAND COMMUNITY UNITED CHURCH OF CHRIST
25100 Skyland Road
Los Gatos, CA 95033-9710
Phone: 408.353.1310

BAPTIST

ANTIOCH BAPTIST CHURCH
268 E Julian Street
San Jose, CA 95112
Phone: 408.295.0066

CHURCH OF THE FOOTHILLS
10160 Clayton Road
San Jose, CA 95127
Phone: 408.258.9592
E-mail: cofsj@aol.com

CROSSWALK COMMUNITY CHURCH
445 S Mary Avenue
Sunnyvale, CA 94086
Phone: 408.736.3120
E-mail: assimilator@crosswalk
   church.com
Web site: www.stthomas-svale.org
Sunday services: 8AM, 10:30AM,
   and 5:30PM
Dress code: CF

EVERGREEN VALLEY BAPTIST CHURCH
2750 Yerba Buena Road
San Jose, CA 95121
Phone: 408.274.7422

FIRST BAPTIST CHURCH
200 Abbott Avenue
Milpitas, CA 95035
Phone: 408.262.0210

FIRST BAPTIST CHURCH
305 N California Avenue
Palo Alto, CA 94301
Phone: 650.327.0561
E-mail: baptistpa@aol.com

GRACE BAPTIST CHURCH
484 E San Fernando Street
San Jose, CA 95112
Phone: 408.295.2035
E-mail: mail@gracechurchsj.org

JERUSALEM BAPTIST CHURCH
398 Sheridan Avenue
Palo Alto, CA 94306
Phone: 650.325.9022

SANTA CLARA FIRST BAPTIST CHURCH
3111 Benton Street
Santa Clara, CA 95051
Phone: 408.241.7635
E-mail: scfbc@aol.com

DISCIPLES OF CHRIST

FIRST CHRISTIAN CHURCH
2890 Middlefield Road
Palo Alto, CA 94306
Phone: 650.327.4188
E-mail: pafcc@aol.com
Web site: members.aol.com
   /pafcc/contact.htm
Sunday service: 11AM
Dress code: SB

FIRST CHRISTIAN CHURCH
80 S Fifth Street
San Jose, CA 95128
Phone: 408.292.2944
Web site: www.firstccsj.org/about.html
Sunday service: 10AM

RAYNOR PARK CHRISTIAN CHURCH
1515 Partridge Avenue
Sunnyvale, CA 94087
Phone: 408.736.8821

ALAMEDA COUNTY

EPISCOPAL

ALL SAINTS' EPISCOPAL CHURCH
911 Dowling Boulevard
San Leandro, CA 94577-2190
Phone: 510.569.7020

ALL SOULS PARISH
2220 Cedar Street
Berkeley, CA 94709-1519
Phone: 510.848.1755
E-mail: allsouls@allsoulsparish.org

CHRIST EPISCOPAL CHURCH
1700 Santa Clara Avenue
Alameda, CA 94501-2515
Phone: 510.523.7200
E-mail: info@christchurchalameda.org
Web site: www.christchurch
alameda.org
Sunday services: 8AM and 10:15AM
Dress code: CF

EPISCOPAL CHURCH OF OUR
SAVIOUR
1011 Harrison Street
Oakland, CA 94607-4426
Phone: 510.834.6447

GOOD SHEPHERD EPISCOPAL
CHURCH
1823 Ninth Street
Berkeley, CA 94710-2102
Phone: 510.549.1433

HOLY CROSS EPISCOPAL CHURCH
19179 Center Street
Castro Valley, CA 94546-3616
Phone: 510.889-7233
E-mail: holycross@yahoo.com
Sunday services: 8:30AM and 10:15AM
Dress code: CF

SAINT ALBAN'S EPISCOPAL CHURCH
1501 Washington Avenue
Albany, CA 94707-1834
Phone: 510.525-1716
E-mail: StAlban153@aol.com
Web site: www.diocal.org/stalbans/
Sunday services: 8AM and 10AM
Dress code: CF

SAINT ANDREW'S EPISCOPAL
CHURCH
5201 Hillen Drive
Oakland, CA 94619-3215
Phone: 510.533.5976

SAINT ANNE'S EPISCOPAL CHURCH
2791 Driscoll Road
Fremont, CA 94539-0324
Phone: 510.490.0553

SAINT AUGUSTINE'S EPISCOPAL
CHURCH
Telegraph Avenue at 29th Street
Oakland, CA 94609-3512
Phone: 510.832.6462
E-mail: info@staugepicopal.org
Web site: www.staugepiscopal.org
Sunday services: 8AM and 10:30AM
Dress code: CF

SAINT BARTHOLOMEW'S
EPISCOPAL CHURCH
678 Enos Way
Livermore, CA 94550-2117
Phone: 925.447.3289
E-mail: saintBarts@aol.com

SAINT CHRISTOPHER'S EPISCOPAL
CHURCH
Via Toledo at Hacienda Avenue
San Lorenzo, CA 94580-0156
Phone: 510.276.7853
E-mail: stchrisepiscopal@yahoo.com
Web site: www.diocal.org
/stchristophers
Sunday services: 8AM and 10:30AM
Dress code: SB

SAINT CLARE'S EPISCOPAL CHURCH
3350 Hopyard Road
Pleasanton, CA 94588-5105
Phone: 925.462.4802
E-mail: stclare@juno.com
Web site: www.stclarescalifornia.com
Sunday services: 8AM, 9:30AM,
and 11AM
Dress code: CF

SAINT CLEMENT'S EPISCOPAL
CHURCH
2837 Claremont Boulevard
Berkeley, CA 94705-1426
Phone: 510.843-2678
E-mail: stclements@earthlink.net
Sunday services: 8AM and 10AM
Dress code: SB

SAINT CUTHBERT'S EPISCOPAL
CHURCH
7932 Mountain Boulevard
Oakland, CA 94605-3799
Phone: 510.635-4949

SAINT JAMES' EPISCOPAL CHURCH
Thornton Avenue at Cabrillo Drive
Fremont, CA 94537-0457
Phone: 510.797.1492
E-mail: stjamespar@aol.com
Sunday services: 8AM, 9AM, and 11AM
Dress code: CF

SAINT JAMES' EPISCOPAL CHURCH
1540 12th Avenue
Oakland, CA 94606-3803
Phone: 510.533.2136
Web site: www.stjamesoakland.
faithweb.com
Sunday services: 8AM and 11AM
Dress code: CF

SAINT JOHN'S EPISCOPAL CHURCH
1707 Gouldin Road
Oakland, CA 94611-2120
Phone: 510.339.2200
E-mail: stjmouse@aol.com
Sunday services: 8AM and 10AM
Dress code: SB and CF

SAINT MARK'S EPISCOPAL CHURCH
2300 Bancroft Way
Berkeley, CA 94704-1604
Phone: 510.848.5107
E-mail: office@stmarksberkeley.org
Web site: www.stmarksberkeley.org
Sunday services: 8AM and 10AM
Dress code: CF

SAINT PAUL'S EPISCOPAL CHURCH
114 Montecito Avenue
Oakland, CA 94610-4556
Phone: 510.834.4314
E-mail: stpauloak@aol.com

LUTHERAN

BETHLEHEM LUTHERAN CHURCH
959 12th Street
Oakland, CA 94607-3233
Phone: 510.452.2245

CHRIST THE KING LUTHERAN
CHURCH
1301 Mowry Avenue
Fremont, CA 94538
Phone: 510.797.3724
E-mail: ctkfrem@inreach.com
Web site: home.inreach.com/ctkfrem/
Sunday services: 8AM and 10:15AM
Dress code: CF

CHRIST LUTHERAN CHURCH
780 Ashbury Avenue
El Cerrito, CA 94530
Phone: 510.524.1050
Web site: members.home.com
/christlutheran
Services: Sunday 10AM, Saturday
5:30PM

FAITH AMERICAN LUTHERAN
CHURCH
4335 Virginia Avenue
Oakland, CA 94619
Phone: 510.895.2286

FAITH LUTHERAN CHURCH
20080 Redwood Road
Castro Valley, CA 94546
Phone: 510.582.0818
Web site: flccv.org
Sunday services: 8AM, 9AM,
and 10:30AM

HOLY TRINITY LUTHERAN
CHURCH
38801 Blacow Road
Fremont, CA 94536
Phone: 510.793.6285
Web site: www.geocities.com
/Heartland/Hills/2025/
Sunday services: 9:30AM

IMMANUEL LUTHERAN CHURCH
1910 Santa Clara Avenue
Alameda, CA 94501
Phone: 510.523.0659

LUTHERAN CHURCH OF THE
CROSS
1744 University Avenue
Berkeley, CA 94703
Phone: 510.848.1424

MESSIAH LUTHERAN CHURCH
25400 Hesperian Boulevard
Hayward, CA 94545
Phone: 510.782.6727

RESURRECTION LUTHERAN
CHURCH
397 Euclid Avenue
Oakland, CA 94610
Phone: 510.444.5382
E-mail: lucyk@pacbell.net
Sunday services: 8AM and 10:30AM
Dress code: CF

SAINT JOHN LUTHERAN CHURCH
1800 55th Avenue
Oakland, CA 94621
Phone: 510.436.6200

SAINT PAUL LUTHERAN CHURCH
1658 Excelsior Avenue
Oakland, CA 94602
Phone: 510.530.6333
E-mail: stpluth@jps.net
Web site: www.jps.net/stpluth
Sunday service: 10AM
Dress code: CF

SHEPHERD OF THE HILLS
LUTHERAN CHURCH
401 Grizzly Peak Boulevard
Berkeley, CA 94708
Phone: 510.524.8281

TRINITY LUTHERAN CHURCH
1323 Central Avenue
Alameda, CA 94501
Phone: 510.522.5220
E-mail: trinityalameda@earthlink.net
Sunday service: 10:30AM
Dress code: CF

TRINITY LUTHERAN CHURCH
650 Alma Avenue
Oakland, CA 94610
Phone: 510.836.3135
Sunday service: 10:15AM
Dress code: CF

UNITED LUTHERAN CHURCH OF
OAKLAND
4100 Mountain Boulevard
Oakland, CA 94619
Phone: 510.531.8050

UNIVERSITY LUTHERAN CHURCH
2425 College Avenue
Berkeley, CA 94704
Phone: 510.843.6230
E-mail: ulc@univelutch.org
Web site: www.univelutch.org
Sunday service: 11AM
Dress code: CF

PRESBYTERIAN

BETHEL COMMUNITY
PRESBYTERIAN CHURCH
14235 Bancroft Avenue
San Leandro, CA 94578
Phone: 510.357.0610
Sunday service: 9:50AM
Dress code: CF

CALVARY PRESBYTERIAN CHURCH
1940 Virginia Street
Berkeley, CA 94709
Phone: 510.848.9132
Web site: www.calpres.wego.com
Sunday service: 10:30AM

CENTERVILLE PRESBYTERIAN
CHURCH
4360 Central Avenue
Fremont, CA 94536
Phone: 510.793.3575
Web site: www.cvpc.org/
Sunday services: 9:30AM and 11AM

CHRIST PRESBYTERIAN CHURCH
890 Fargo Avenue
San Leandro, CA 94579
Phone: 510.351.8534
E-mail: cpc890fgo@aol.com
Sunday services: 9:30AM
Dress code: PC

COLLEGE AVENUE PRESBYTERIAN
CHURCH
5951 College Avenue
Oakland, CA 94618
Phone: 510.658.3665

ELMHURST PRESBYTERIAN
CHURCH
1332 98th Avenue
Oakland, CA 94603
Phone: 510.568.7861

FAITH PRESBYTERIAN CHURCH
430 49th Street
Oakland, CA 94609
Phone: 510.653.9752

FIRST PRESBYTERIAN CHURCH
2001 Santa Clara Avenue
Alameda, CA 94501
Phone: 510.522.1477
E-mail: office@fpcalameda.org
Web site: www.fpcalameda.org
Sunday service: 10:30AM

FIRST PRESBYTERIAN CHURCH
2407 Dana Street
Berkeley, CA 94704
Phone: 510.848.6242
Web site: www.fpcberkeley.org
Sunday services: 9:15AM, 10:45AM,
and 5:45PM

FIRST PRESBYTERIAN CHURCH
2490 Grove Way
Hayward, CA 94546
Phone: 510.581.6203
Web site: www.fpch.net
Sunday services: 9AM and 10:30AM

FIRST PRESBYTERIAN CHURCH
2020 Fifth Street
Livermore, CA 94550
Phone: 925.447.2078
E-mail: fpclvrmr@pacbell.net
Web site: www.fpc-livermore
.org/index.html
Sunday services: 9AM and 10:30AM

FIRST PRESBYTERIAN CHURCH
35450 Newark Boulevard
Newark, CA 94560
Phone: 510.797.8811
E-mail: fpcn_darryl@iflashcom.com
Sunday services: 8:30AM and 11:15AM
Dress code: CF

FIRST PRESBYTERIAN CHURCH
2619 Broadway
Oakland, CA 94612
Phone: 510.444.3555
Sunday service: 10AM
Dress code: SB

FIRST PRESBYTERIAN CHURCH
180 Estudillo Avenue
San Leandro, CA 94577
Phone: 510.483.2772
Sunday service: 9:30AM
Dress code: CF

FRUITVALE PRESBYTERIAN
CHURCH
2735 MacArthur Boulevard
Oakland, CA 94602
Phone: 510.530.0915
E-mail: fvpc@cwnet.com
Web site: www.fvpc.org
Sunday service: 11AM

HIGH STREET PRESBYTERIAN
CHURCH
1941 High Street
Oakland, CA 94601
Phone: 510.533.2366

HILLSIDE PRESBYTERIAN CHURCH
2708 Ritchie Street
Oakland, CA 94605
Phone: 510.568.2032

JOHN KNOX PRESBYTERIAN
CHURCH
7421 Amarillo Road
Dublin, CA 94568
Phone: 925.828.1846

MONTCLAIR PRESBYTERIAN
CHURCH
5701 Thornhill Drive
Oakland, CA 94611
Phone: 510.339.1131

MOUNT EDEN PRESBYTERIAN
CHURCH
26236 Adrian Avenue
Hayward, CA 94545
Phone: 650.786.9333

NEW COVENANT PRESBYTERIAN
CHURCH
890 Fargo Avenue
San Leandro, CA 94579
Phone: 510.352.9935

PARK BOULEVARD PRESBYTERIAN
CHURCH
4101 Park Boulevard
Oakland, CA 94602
Phone: 510.530.5311
E-mail: office@pbpc.org
Web site: www.pbpc.org/
Sunday service: 10:30AM

PLEASANTON PRESBYTERIAN
CHURCH
4300 Mirador Drive
Pleasanton, CA 94566
Phone: 925.846.4436
Web site: www.pleasantonpres.org
Sunday services: 9AM and 10:30AM

SAINT JOHNS PRESBYTERIAN
CHURCH
2727 College Avenue
Berkeley, CA 94705
Phone: 510.845.6830
E-mail: sjpcberkeley@aol.com
Web site: www.stjohns
.presbychurch.net
Sunday service: 10AM

WESTMINSTER HILLS
PRESBYTERIAN CHURCH
27269 Patrick Avenue
Hayward, CA 94544
Phone: 510.782.5795

METHODIST

ALBANY UNITED METHODIST
CHURCH
980 Stannage Avenue
Albany, CA 94706
Phone: 510.526.7346
Sunday service: 10AM
Dress code: PC

ASBURY UNITED METHODIST
CHURCH
4743 East Avenue
Livermore, CA 94550
Phone: 925.447-1950
E-mail: info@asburylive.org
Web site: www.asburylive.org
Sunday services: 9AM and 10:45AM
Dress code: CF

BUENA VISTA UNITED METHODIST
CHURCH
2311 Buena Vista Avenue
Alameda, CA 94501
Phone: 510.522.2688

CASTRO VALLEY UNITED
METHODIST CHURCH
19806 Wisteria Street
Castro Valley, CA 94546
Phone: 510.581.3486

COURT STREET UNITED
METHODIST CHURCH
3005 Van Buren Street
Alameda, CA 94501
Phone: 510.523.6525

DOWNS MEMORIAL UNITED
METHODIST CHURCH
6026 Idaho Street
Oakland, CA 94608
Phone: 510.654.5858

ELMHURST UNITED METHODIST
CHURCH
1659 83rd Avenue
Oakland, CA 94621
Phone: 510.568.1484

EPWORTH UNITED METHODIST
CHURCH
1953 Hopkins Street
Berkeley, CA 94707
Phone: 510.524.2921

FAITH UNITED METHODIST
CHURCH
788 Lewelling Boulevard
San Leandro, CA 94579
Phone: 510.357.5484

FIRST UNITED METHODIST
CHURCH
2950 Washington Boulevard
Fremont, CA 94539
Phone: 510.490.0200

FIRST UNITED METHODIST
CHURCH
1183 B Street
Hayward, CA 94541
Phone: 510.581.2266

FIRST UNITED METHODIST
CHURCH
1600 Bancroft Avenue
San Leandro, CA 94577
Phone: 510.483.0606

LAKE MERRITT UNITED
METHODIST CHURCH
1255 First Avenue
Oakland, CA 94606
Phone: 510.465.4793
Web site: www.lakemerrittumc.com
Sunday service: 10:30AM
Dress code: CF

LAKE PARK UNITED METHODIST
CHURCH
281 Santa Clara Avenue
Oakland, CA 94610
Phone: 510.444.7262

LAUREL UNITED METHODIST
CHURCH
3525 Kansas Avenue
Oakland, CA 94619
Phone: 510.531.7613

LYNNEWOOD UNITED METHODIST
CHURCH
4444 Black Avenue
Pleasanton, CA 94566
Phone: 925.846.0221

MELROSE UNITED METHODIST
CHURCH
1655 54th Avenue
Oakland, CA 94601
Phone: 510.532.3800
Sunday service: 10:45AM
Dress code: SB

MONTCLAIR UNITED METHODIST
CHURCH
2162 Mountain Boulevard
Oakland, CA 94611
Phone: 510.531.8208

SAINT PAUL UNITED METHODIST
CHURCH
33350 Peace Terrace
Fremont, CA 94555
Phone: 415.429.3990

SHATTUCK AVENUE UNITED
METHODIST CHURCH
6300 Shattuck Avenue
Oakland, CA 94609
Phone: 510.653.4028

TAYLOR MEMORIAL UNITED
METHODIST CHURCH
1188 12th Street
Oakland, CA 94607
Phone: 510.444.6162

TRINITY UNITED METHODIST
CHURCH
2362 Bancroft Way
Berkeley, CA 94704
Phone: 510.548.4716
Web site: www.trinityberkeley.org
Sunday service: 10:30AM
Dress code: PC

TWIN TOWERS UNITED
METHODIST CHURCH
1411 Oak Street
Alameda, CA 94501
Phone: 510.522.6744

WESLEY UNITED METHODIST
CHURCH
628 Schafer Road
Hayward, CA 94544
Phone: 510.782.5383

UNITED METHODIST CHURCH
1710 Carleton Street
Berkeley, CA 94703
Phone: 510.848.4680

UNITED CHURCH OF CHRIST

ARLINGTON COMMUNITY UNITED
CHURCH OF CHRIST
52 Arlington Avenue
Kensington, CA 94707-1099
Phone: 510.526.9146

BROADMOOR COMMUNITY UNITED
CHURCH OF CHRIST
301 Dowling Boulevard
San Leandro, CA 94577-1931
Phone: 510.568.0402

COMMUNITY UNITED CHURCH OF
CHRIST
831 W Grand Avenue
Oakland, CA 94607
Phone: 510.451.2398

CONGREGATIONAL UNITED
CHURCH OF CHRIST
38255 Blacow Road
Fremont, CA 94536-7113
Phone: 510.793.3970
E-mail: fremontcc@mindspring.com
Sunday service: 10AM
Dress code: CF

EDEN UNITED CHURCH OF CHRIST
21455 Birch Street
Hayward, CA 94541-2131
Phone: 510.582.9533
E-mail: edenucc@msn.com
Web site: www.thinkingchurch.org
Sunday service: 10AM
Dress code: CF

FIRST CONGREGATIONAL UNITED
CHURCH OF CHRIST
1912 Central Avenue
Alameda, CA 94501
Phone: 510.522.6012
E-mail:
fcc.ucc.alameda@worldnet.att.net
Sunday service: 10:30AM
Dress code: CF

FIRST CONGREGATIONAL UNITED
CHURCH OF CHRIST
2345 Channing Way
Berkeley, CA 94704-2280
Phone: 510.848.3696
E-mail: firstberk@aol.com
Web site: www.fccb.org
Sunday service: 10AM
Dress code: CF

FIRST CONGREGATIONAL UNITED
CHURCH OF CHRIST
2501 Harrison Street
Oakland, CA 94612-3899
Phone: 510.444.8511
E-mail: fcc_oakland@juno.com
Sunday service: 10AM
Dress code: CF

NEW SPIRIT COMMUNITY CHURCH
1798 Scenic Avenue
Berkeley, CA 94709
Phone: 510.849.8280
E-mail: admin@newspiritchurch.org
Web site: www.newspiritchurch.org
Sunday service: 11AM
Dress code: CF

NILES CONGREGATIONAL UNITED
CHURCH OF CHRIST
Corner of H Street at Third Street
Fremont, CA 94536-0265
Phone: 510.797.0895
Web site: www.nileschurch.org
Sunday service: 10AM
Dress code: CF

PILGRIM CONGREGATIONAL
UNITED CHURCH OF CHRIST
5763 Walnut Street
Oakland, CA 94605-1050
Phone: 510.430.0141

PLYMOUTH UNITED CHURCH OF
CHRIST
424 Monte Vista Avenue
Oakland, CA 94611-4570
Phone: 510.654.5300
Sunday service: 11AM
Dress code: CF

SAN LEANDRO COMMUNITY
CHURCH
1395 Bancroft Avenue
San Leandro, CA 94577
Phone: 510.483.1811
Web site: www.slcommunity
church.com/

SAN LORENZO COMMUNITY
CHURCH UNITED CHURCH OF
CHRIST
945 Paseo Grande
San Lorenzo, CA 94580-0031
Phone: 510.276.4808
Sunday service: 10AM
Dress code: CF

SKYLINE COMMUNITY UNITED
CHURCH OF CHRIST
12540 Skyline Boulevard
Oakland, CA 94619-3127
Phone: 510.531.8212
E-mail: skylineucc@yahoo.com
Sunday service: 10AM
Dress code: CF

SOUTH BERKELEY COMMUNITY
CHURCH
1802 Fairview Street
Berkeley, CA 94703-2414
Phone: 510.652.1040
Sunday service: 11AM
Dress code: CF

UNITED CHURCH OF HAYWARD
UNITED CHURCH OF CHRIST
30540 Mission Boulevard
Hayward, CA 94544-7496
Phone: 510.471.4452

BAPTIST

ALLEN TEMPLE BAPTIST CHURCH
501 International Boulevard
Oakland, CA 94621
Phone: 510.569.9418

BETH EDEN BAPTIST CHURCH
1183 10th Street
Oakland, CA 94607
Phone: 510.444.1625
E-mail: church@betheden.com
Web site: www.betheden.com
Sunday services: 11AM and 6PM
Dress code: SB

CANAAN CHRISTIAN COVENANT
5782 Foothill Boulevard
Oakland, CA 94605
Phone: 510.636.1881

CHURCH OF GOOD SHEPHERD
799 52nd Street
Oakland, CA 94609
Phone: 510.653.6055

CHURCH BY THE SIDE OF THE
ROAD
2108 Russell Street
Berkeley, CA 94705
Phone: 510.644.1263

THE CHURCH WITHOUT WALLS
534 22nd Street
Oakland, CA 94612
Phone: 510.869.3927

COMMUNITY CHURCH
26555 Gading Road
Hayward, CA 94544
Phone: 510.782.8593

COSMOPOLITAN BAPTIST CHURCH
988 85th Avenue
Oakland, CA 94624
Phone: 510.635.5275

FAITH BAPTIST CHURCH
2680 64th Avenue
Oakland, CA 94605
Phone: 510.633.1628

FIRST BAPTIST CHURCH
1515 Santa Clara Avenue
Alameda, CA 94501
Phone: 510.522.9243
E-mail: info@firstbaptistalameda.org

FIRST BAPTIST CHURCH
1319 Solano Avenue
Albany, CA 94706
Phone: 510.526.6632

FIRST BAPTIST CHURCH
18550 Redwood Road
Castro Valley, CA 94546
Phone: 510.582.0515

FIRST BAPTIST CHURCH
534 22nd Street
Oakland, CA 94612
Phone: 510.832.4326
Web site: www.best.com/snc/
Sunday service: 11AM
Dress code: varied

IMANI BAPTIST CHURCH
10205 MacArthur Boulevard
Oakland, CA 94605
Phone: 510.568.3887

IMANI COMMUNITY CHURCH
3300 MacArthur Boulevard
Oakland, CA 94602
Phone: 510.531.5411

LIBERTY HILL MISSIONARY
997 University Avenue
Berkeley, CA 94710
Phone: 510.848.3855

MARTIN LUTHER KING BAPTIST
CHURCH
3003 School Street
Oakland, CA 94602
Phone: 510.532.8111

MCGEE AVENUE CHURCH
1640 Stuart Street
Berkeley, CA 94703
Phone: 510.843.1774

NEW LIFE CHRISTIAN FELLOWSHIP
22360 Redwood Road
Castro Valley, CA 94546
Phone: 925.582-2261

PARADISE BAPTIST CHURCH
9670 Empire Road
Oakland, CA 94603
Phone: 510.562.8370

SAN LEANDRO COMMUNITY
CHURCH
1395 Bancroft Avenue
San Leandro, CA 94577
Phone: 510.483.1811
Sunday service: 11AM
Dress code: PC

SAN LORENZO BAPTIST CHURCH
180 Lewelling Boulevard
San Lorenzo, CA 94580
Phone: 510.278.2622
E-mail: sanlorenzobp@earthlink.net

THORNTON AVENUE BAPTIST
CHURCH
500 Thornton Avenue
Fremont, CA 94536
Phone: 510.797.7910

THOUSAND OAKS BAPTIST CHURCH
821 Catalina Avenue
Berkeley, CA 94707
Phone: 510.526.3773

WESTERN CONTRA
COSTA COUNTY

EPISCOPAL

HOLY TRINITY EPISCOPAL CHURCH
555 37th Street
Richmond, CA 94805-2272
Phone: 510.232.7896

LUTHERAN

GRACE LUTHERAN CHURCH
2369 Barrett Avenue
Richmond, CA 94804
Phone: 510.235.3858

HOPE LUTHERAN CHURCH
2830 May Road
El Sobrante, CA 94803
Phone: 510.222.6394
E-mail: Gruebmeyer@aol.com
Web site: www.hopelutheranchurch
.homestead.com
Sunday services: 8:30AM and 10:45AM
Dress code: CF

SAINT JAMES LUTHERAN CHURCH
1963 Carlson Boulevard
Richmond, CA 94804
Phone: 510.524.4616
Sunday service: 11AM

PRESBYTERIAN

NORTHMINSTER PRESBYTERIAN CHURCH
545 Ashbury Avenue
El Cerrito, CA 94530
Phone: 510.524.4401
Sunday service: 11AM
Dress code: CF

METHODIST

EL CERRITO UNITED METHODIST CHURCH
6830 Stockton Avenue
El Cerrito, CA 94530
Phone: 510.525.3500

EL SOBRANTE UNITED METHODIST CHURCH
670 Appian Way
El Sobrante, CA 94803
Phone: 510.223.0790

FIRST UNITED METHODIST CHURCH
201 Martina Street
Richmond, CA 94801
Phone: 510.236.0527

GOOD SHEPHERD UNITED METHODIST CHURCH
6226 Arlington Boulevard
Richmond, CA 94805
Phone: 510.232.4043

SAINT LUKE'S UNITED METHODIST CHURCH
3200 Barrett Avenue
Richmond, CA 94804
Phone: 510.234.5263

UNITED CHURCH OF CHRIST

MIRA VISTA UNITED CHURCH OF CHRIST
7075 Cutting Boulevard
El Cerrito, CA 94530-1800
Phone: 510.234.0110
E-mail: miravista@juno.com
Web site: miravistaucc.org
Sunday service: 10AM

BAPTIST

FIRST BAPTIST CHURCH
777 Sonoma Street
Richmond, CA 94805
Phone: 510.234.4395
E-mail: fbc@worldchristian.net

NEW LIFE CHURCH
770 Sonoma Street
Richmond, CA 94805
Phone: 510.234.4395
Web site: www.newlifeinjesus.net
Sunday service: 10:30AM
Dress code: CF

TEMPLE BAPTIST CHURCH
1960 Carlson Boulevard
Richmond, CA 94804
Phone: 510.525.9103

MARIN COUNTY

EPISCOPAL

CHRIST EPISCOPAL CHURCH
70 Santa Rosa Avenue at San Carlos
Avenue
Sausalito, CA 94966-0005
Phone: 415.332.1539
E-mail: maschurch@aol.com
Web site: christchurchsausalito.org
Sunday services: 8AM and 10AM
Dress code: CF

**CHURCH OF THE HOLY
INNOCENTS**
2 Tamalpais Drive
Corte Madera, CA 94925-0005
Phone: 415.924.4393
Sunday services: 7:45AM, 10AM,
and 11:30AM
Dress code: CF

**EPISCOPAL CHURCH OF THE
NATIVITY**
333 Ellen Drive
San Rafael, CA 94903-4239
Phone: 415.479.7023

**EPISCOPAL CHURCH OF THE
REDEEMER**
123 Knight Drive
San Rafael, CA 94901-1427
Phone: 415.456.0508

OUR SAVIOUR EPISCOPAL CHURCH
10 Old Mill Street
Mill Valley, CA 94941-1894
Phone: 415.388.1907

**SAINT AIDAN'S EPISCOPAL
CHURCH**
30 Brighton Road
Bolinas, CA 94924-0629
Phone: 415.868.9802
Sunday service: 10AM
Dress code: PC

**SAINT COLUMBA EPISCOPAL
CHURCH & RETREAT HOUSE**
Sir Francis Drake Boulevard
Inverness, CA 94937
Phone: 415.669.1039
E-mail: saintcolumba@earthlink.net
Sunday service: 10AM
Dress code: CF and PC

**SAINT FRANCIS OF ASSISI
EPISCOPAL CHURCH**
967 Fifth Street
Novato, CA 94945-3105
Phone: 415.892.1609
E-mail: stfranc@gte.net
Web site: www.stfrancisnovato.com
Sunday services: 7:30AM, 8:50AM,
and 10:30AM
Dress code: CF and PC

SAINT JOHN'S EPISCOPAL CHURCH
Lagunitas Road and Shady Lane
Ross, CA 94957-0217
Phone: 415.456.1102
E-mail: stjohns@jps.net
Web site: www.jps.net.stjohns
Sunday services: 8AM and 10AM;
5PM on first Sunday of month
Dress code: SB

SAINT PAUL'S EPISCOPAL CHURCH
1123 Court Street
San Rafael, CA 94901-2909
Phone: 415.456.4842

SAINT STEPHEN'S EPISCOPAL
CHURCH
3 Bay View Avenue
Belvedere, CA 94920-0097
Phone: 415.435.4501
E-mail: jimward@ststephenschurch.org
Web site: www.ststephenschurch.org
Sunday services: 8AM and 10AM
Dress code: CF

LUTHERAN

ALL SAINTS LUTHERAN CHURCH
2 San Marin Drive
Novato, CA 94945
Phone: 415.892.1669
E-mail: aslc@gte.net

CHRIST THE VICTOR LUTHERAN
CHURCH
2626 Sir Francis Drake Boulevard
Fairfax, CA 94930
Phone: 415.454.6365
E-mail: christthevictor@mail
andnews.com
Sunday service: 10:30AM
Dress code: CF

FAITH LUTHERAN CHURCH
355 Los Ranchitos Road
San Rafael (Terra Linda), CA 94903
Phone: 415.479.4541
E-mail: faithLC@aol.com
Sunday service: 10:30AM
Dress code: CF

MARIN LUTHERAN CHURCH
649 Meadowsweet Drive
Corte Madera, CA 94925
Phone: 415.924.3782
Web site: www.marinlutheran.com
Sunday services: 8:45AM and 11AM

SHEPHERD OF THE HILLS
LUTHERAN CHURCH
9 Shepherd Way
Tiburon, CA 94920
Phone: 415.435.1528

PRESBYTERIAN

CHRIST PRESBYTERIAN CHURCH
IN TERRA LINDA
620 Del Ganado Road
San Rafael, CA 94903
Phone: 415.479.2712
Sunday service: 9:30AM
Dress code: CF

COMMUNITY PRESBYTERIAN
CHURCH
6001 Sir Francis Drake Boulevard
PO Box 98
San Geronimo, CA 94963
Phone: 415.488.9318

COMMUNITY PRESBYTERIAN
CHURCH
32 Belvedere Avenue
Stinson Beach, CA 94970
Phone: 415.868.2603

FIRST PRESBYTERIAN CHURCH
72 Kensington Road
San Anselmo, CA 94960
Phone: 415.456.3713
E-mail: mail@togetherweserve.org
Web site: www.togetherweserve.org
Sunday service: 10AM

FIRST PRESBYTERIAN CHURCH
1510 Fifth Avenue
San Rafael, CA 94901
Phone: 415.456.6760

FIRST PRESBYTERIAN CHURCH
112 Bulkley Avenue
Sausalito, CA 94965
Phone: 415.332.3790

NOVATO PRESBYTERIAN CHURCH
710 Wilson Avenue
Novato, CA 94947
Phone: 415.897.6152

POINT REYES COMMUNITY
PRESBYTERIAN CHURCH
Box 487, Highway 1
Point Reyes Station, CA 94956
Phone: 415.663.1349

REDWOODS PRESBYTERIAN CHURCH
110 Magnolia Avenue
Larkspur, CA 94939
Phone: 415.924.4832
E-mail: redwoodschurch@
mindspring.com
Web site: www.forministry.com
/94939RPC
Sunday services: 10:30AM and 5:30PM
Dress code: CF

SAINT ANDREW UNITED
PRESBYTERIAN CHURCH
101 Donahue Street
Marin City, CA 94966
Phone: 415.332.1011

SAINT LUKE PRESBYTERIAN
CHURCH
10 Bayview Drive
San Rafael, CA 94901
Phone: 415.454.2705

SLEEPY HOLLOW PRESBYTERIAN
CHURCH
100 Tarry Road
San Anselmo, CA 94960
Phone: 415.453.8221
E-mail: SHPchurch@aol.com
Sunday service: 9:30AM
Dress code: CF

WESTMINSTER PRESBYTERIAN
CHURCH/RICHARDSON BAY
PRESBYTERIAN
240 Tiburon Boulevard
Tiburon, CA 94920
Phone: 415.383.5272

METHODIST

ALDERSGATE UNITED METHODIST
CHURCH
1 Wellbrock Heights
San Rafael, CA 94903
Phone: 415.492.0237

FIRST UNITED METHODIST CHURCH
9 Ross Valley Road
San Rafael, CA 94901
Phone: 415.453.8716
E-mail: 1stumc@aol.com
Web site: www.ruah.net
/unitedmethodist
Sunday service: 11AM
Dress code: CF

MOUNT TAMALPAIS UNITED
METHODIST CHURCH
410 Sycamore Avenue
Mill Valley, CA 94941
Phone: 415.388.4456

NOVATO UNITED METHODIST
CHURCH
1473 S Novato Boulevard
Novato, CA 94947
Phone: 415.892.9896

UNITED CHURCH OF CHRIST

COMMUNITY CHURCH OF MILL
VALLEY
8 Olive Street
Mill Valley, CA 94941-1853
Phone: 415.388.5540
E-mail: ccmvucc@aol.com
Web site: millvalleyucc.org
Sunday service: 10:30AM
Dress code: SB

COMMUNITY CONGREGATIONAL
CHURCH OF BELVEDERE-TIBURON
145 Rock Hill Drive
Tiburon, CA 94920-1452
Phone: 415.435.9108
Sunday services: 7:30AM and 10AM
Dress code: CF

FAIRFAX COMMUNITY CHURCH
2398 Sir Francis Drake Boulevard
Fairfax, CA 94930-1127
Phone: 415.454.6085
E-mail: FairfaxUCC@aol.com
Sunday service: 10:30AM
Dress code: CF and PC

FIRST CONGREGATIONAL UNITED
CHURCH OF CHRIST
8 N San Pedro Road
San Rafael, CA 94903-4007
Phone: 415.479.2747

BAPTIST

HILLSIDE CHURCH OF MARIN
5461 Paradise Drive
Corte Madera, CA 94925
Phone: 415.924.2297

BETHEL BAPTIST CHURCH
1929 Novato Boulevard
Novato, CA 94947
Phone: 415.892.3268

MILLER AVENUE CHURCH
285 Miller Avenue
Mill Valley, CA 94941
Phone: 415.388.5993

VILLAGE BAPTIST CHURCH
825 Drake Avenue
Marin City, CA 94965
Phone: 415.332.5156

Alternatives to Mainline
Denominations

Following is information on location and service times for three non-mainline churches that are mentioned earlier in Part Two: Metropolitan Community Churches, which appear in Chapter Five, and Unitarian Universalists and Quakers, both discussed in Chapter Six. Listings are sorted first by denomination, then by region (San Francisco, East Bay, South Bay, North Bay). Within a region, the churches are listed in alphabetical order. Some of the information is from denominational web sites.

METROPOLITAN COMMUNITY CHURCHES

SAN FRANCISCO

METROPOLITAN COMMUNITY
CHURCH OF SAN FRANCISCO
150 Eureka Street
San Francisco, CA 94114
Phone: 415.863.4434
E-mail: MCCSF@aol.com
Web site: www.mccsf.org
Sunday services:
9AM: traditional
11AM: traditional with choral music
7PM: high-energy service with pop
and gospel music
Other services: Wednesday, 7PM, Taizé

EAST BAY

METROPOLITAN COMMUNITY
CHURCH OF GREATER HAYWARD
100 Hacienda
San Lorenzo, CA 94580
Phone: 510.481.9720
E-mail: bearofmcc@aol.com
Web site:
www.capybara.com/MCCGH
Sunday service: 12:30PM (in Christ
Lutheran Church at 100 Hacienda)

NEW LIFE METROPOLITAN
COMMUNITY CHURCH
1823 Ninth Street
Berkeley, CA 94710-2102
Phone: 510.843.9355
E-mail: revbarry@home.com
Web site:
www.members.aol.com/MCCPages/
NewLife.htm/
Sunday service: 12:30PM

NEW SPIRIT METROPOLITAN
COMMUNITY CHURCH
1798 Scenic Avenue
Berkeley, CA 94709
Phone: 510.849.8280
E-mail: revkfoster@aol.com
Sunday service: 11AM in the Pacific
School of Religion chapel

SOUTH BAY

METROPOLITAN COMMUNITY
CHURCH SAN JOSE
65 South Seventh Street
(between Santa Clara and San
Fernando), San Jose
Phone: 408.279.2711
E-mail: mccsj@flash.net
Web site: www.flash.net
/~mccsj/index.htm
Sunday service: 10:30AM

UNITARIAN UNIVERSALIST CHURCHES

SAN FRANCISCO

FIRST UNITARIAN UNIVERSALIST
SOCIETY OF SAN FRANCISCO
1187 Franklin Street
San Francisco, CA 94109
Phone: 415.776.4580
E-mail: church@uusf.org
Web site: www.uusf.org
Sunday service: 11AM

EAST BAY

BERKELEY FELLOWSHIP OF
UNITARIAN UNIVERSALISTS
1606 Bonita Avenue
Berkeley, CA 94707
Phone: 510.841.4824
E-mail: bfuu@juno.com

FIRST UNITARIAN CHURCH OF
OAKLAND
685 14th Street (at Castro)
Oakland, CA 94612
Phone: 510.893.6129
E-mail: uu@fuco.org
Sunday services: 9:15 and 11AM

MISSION PEAK UNITARIAN
UNIVERSALIST CONGREGATION
Tri-Cities Children's Center,
43100 Isle Royal, Fremont
Phone: 510.252.1477
E-mail: MPUUCONG@aol.com
Web site: www.members.
  aol.com/mpuuc/
Sunday service: 10AM

STARR KING UNITARIAN
UNIVERSALIST CHURCH
22577 Bayview Avenue
Hayward, CA 94541
Phone: 510.581.2060
Sunday service: 10:45AM

UNITARIAN UNIVERSALIST
CHURCH OF BERKELEY
1 Lawson Road
Kensington, CA 94707
Phone: 510.525.0302
E-mail: uucb@uucb.org
Web site: www.uucb.org
Sunday service: 10:45AM

SOUTH BAY

FIRST UNITARIAN CHURCH OF
SAN JOSE
160 N Third Street
San Jose, CA 95112
Phone: 408.292.3858
E-mail: fucsj@sanjoseuu.org
Web site: www.sanjoseuu.org
Sunday services: 9:30 (Spanish
language) and 11AM

UNITARIAN FELLOWSHIP OF LOS
GATOS
15980 Blossom Hill Road
Los Gatos, CA 95032
Phone: 408.358.1212
E-mail: contact@lguf.org
Web site: www.lguf.org
Sunday service: 10:30AM

UNITARIAN UNIVERSALIST
FELLOWSHIP
2124 Brewster Avenue (at Lowell
Street)
Redwood City, CA 94062
Phone: 650.365.6913
E-mail: office@uufrc.org
Sunday service: 10:30AM

UNITARIAN UNIVERSALIST
FELLOWSHIP OF SUNNYVALE
Congregational Community Church
1112 Bernardo Avenue
Sunnyvale, CA
Phone: 408.739.0549
E-mail: info@uufs.org
Sunday services: 9:15AM and 11AM

UNITARIAN UNIVERSALISTS
OF SAN MATEO
300 E Santa Inez Avenue (corner of
Ellsworth)
San Mateo, CA 94401
Phone: 650.342.5946
E-mail: uusmchr@aol.com
Web site: www.uusm.net
Sunday services: 9 and 11AM

NORTH BAY

UNITARIAN UNIVERSALIST
CONGREGATION OF MARIN
240 Channing Way
San Rafael, CA 94903
Phone: 415.479.4131
E-mail: uucm@slip.net
Web site: www.slip.net/~uucm
Sunday services: 9:30 and 11AM

QUAKER MEETINGS

SAN FRANCISCO

NOE/BERNAL WORSHIP GROUP
*(affiliated with San Francisco Monthly
Meeting)*
65 Ninth Street
San Francisco, CA 94103
Phone: 415.641.7467
Worship service: Sundays at 9:30AM

SAN FRANCISCO MONTHLY
MEETING
65 Ninth Street
San Francisco, CA 94103
Phone: 415.431.7440
Web site: www.geocities.com/
WestHollywood/2473/sfmtg.html
Worship service: Sundays at 11AM

EAST BAY

BERKELEY FRIENDS CHURCH
*This congregation is in the "programmed"
tradition and has a pastor who leads the
worship.*
1600 Sacramento Street (at Cedar)
Berkeley, CA 94702
Phone: 510.524.4112
Web site: users.lmi.net/friends/
index.html
Worship service: Sundays at 11AM

BERKELEY MONTHLY MEETING
2151 Vine Street (at Walnut)
Berkeley, CA 94709
Phone: 510.843.9725
Web site: www.quaker.org/berkmm/
Worship service: Sundays at 11AM

STRAWBERRY CREEK MONTHLY
MEETING
Mailing address: PO Box 5065,
Berkeley, CA 94705
Phone: 510.524.9186
Worship service: Sundays at 10AM at
the Crowden School,
1475 Rose Street (at Sacramento)

SOUTH BAY

PALO ALTO MONTHLY MEETING
957 Colorado Avenue
Palo Alto, CA 94303
Phone: 650.856.0744
Worship service: Sundays at 10:30AM

SAN JOSE MONTHLY MEETING
1041 Morse Street
San Jose, CA 95126
Phone: 408.251.0408
Web site: www-acc.scu.edu/
~akoster/sjfriends.htm
Worship service: Sundays at 10AM

NORTH BAY

MARIN MONTHLY MEETING
Mailing address: PO Box 1301, Mill
Valley, CA 94942
Phone: 415.435.5755
Worship service: Sundays at 10AM at
177 E Blithedale, Mill Valley

WEST MARIN WORSHIP GROUP
*(affiliated with San Francisco Monthly
Meeting)*
Phone: 415.448.9795 or
415.398.7229
Worship service: Sundays at 11:30AM
in the Point Reyes Presbyterian
Church on Highway 1 in Point Reyes
Station

Afterword

We were born to manifest the glory of God that is within us.
It's not just in some of us; it's in everyone. And as we let our own light shine,
we unconsciously give other people permission to do the same. As we are
liberated from our own fear, our presence automatically liberates others.

—NELSON MANDELA

I once attended a workshop given by a consultant who is something of a legend in local nonprofit circles. The presenter was making some point related to the fact that people respond better when they can see evidence that other people are pitching in, too. "Think about how churches take up a collection," she said. It would save quite a few steps to pass the plates from the back to the front, but the ushers start at the front so that everyone watches the plates being passed. Brilliant!" She pointed out that churches also excel at finding and motivating volunteers, another challenge of perennial concern to nonprofits. She finished with the observation, "Well, of course churches are good at all this, they've had centuries to figure it out!"

That comment triggered a small epiphany for me about my church experience. I joined a mainline Protestant denomination for reasons unrelated to finding the answers I had been seeking, alone, for years: Why am I here? How can I be a force for good in the world? What is the path my life should take? I soon found out how much more effectively the work of wrestling with big questions is accomplished in the company of others. I also discovered that the Anglican (like the Presbyterian, Methodist, Lutheran, Baptist, and UCC) tradition puts an impressive store of powerful spiritual equipment at your disposal. Churches have, indeed, been working on it for centuries.

"Well, duh!" you might say if you have never been disaffected from organized religion. But I believe this is real news for heathens. For most of my adult life I have seen the mainstream American experience as a wallpaper of activities that vast quantities of people do all the time yet I wouldn't be caught dead at. For a long time I put church-going in that category, along with shopping at Wal-Mart and eating at ChuckECheese.

I am delighted to have found out that I was wrong. I hope this book will lead you to a similarly happy discovery.

GLOSSARY

This glossary is intended as a guide to understanding some of the unfamiliar words you may encounter in your reading of this book. Many of the words included here have technical definitions in church circles, but I have only defined the terms in the broader sense in which I have used them.

A-B 🎵

AFFIRMING. See Welcoming.

ANGLICAN applies to churches that are part of the Anglican Communion, the worldwide association of churches that developed from the original Church of England. The Episcopal Church in the United States is an Anglican church.

C 🎵

CLERGY is a generic term that refers to all ordained persons.

COFFEE HOUR is the word many congregations use for the social time after a worship service. See also Fellowship.

COMMUNION is also known as Holy Communion, Holy Eucharist, Lord's Supper, the Divine Liturgy, the Mass, and the Great Offering. The most commonly celebrated sacrament in the life of most Christians, the Eucharist is at the heart of the Sunday worship service in some denominations.

CONFERENCE is the local level of church authority in the United Church of Christ. The local UCC churches belong to the Northern California Nevada Conference.

CONGREGATION means an individual church; in that sense of the word, I use it interchangeably with parish throughout this book. The word congregation can also be used as a collective noun for the lay members of a church.

COVENANT is a two-way promise, such as the Biblical one that God made with the Hebrews that he would protect them and they would follow God's laws.

CREED is a formal statement of the chief articles of Christian belief, such as the Apostles' Creed, the Nicene Creed, or the Athanasian Creed. Different denominations will have official positions on which, if any, of these ancient creeds they subscribe to. Many church services include the saying of one of these creeds, or another statement of belief, by the congregation together.

D

DENOMINATION is a national church, a group of churches across the country from the same tradition that share a national governing structure. The ECLA (Evangelical Lutheran Church in America) is a denomination. The word is also used loosely to apply to several national churches that come from the same tradition—for example, you might hear people talk about the Lutheran denomination, which would include both the ELCA and the Lutheran Church Missouri Synod, which has its own, separate national church and governing structure.

DIOCESE is the local level of church authority in the Episcopal Church. The local dioceses are the Diocese of California and the Diocese of El Camino Real.

DISTRICT is the local level of church authority in the United Methodist Church. The local UMC districts are the Golden Gate District and the Bayview District.

E–F

ELDER is the word Presbyterians use for the elected lay leaders in their churches.

FAITH COMMUNITY is a generic and marvelously PC phrase that includes churches, temples, zendos, and other religious meeting places.

FELLOWSHIP is an umbrella term for getting together to have fun and/or get to know each other better. The little social times offered after Sunday service are called "fellowship hour" at many churches. Youth programs often have "fellowship" outings or activities, which offer a chance for the kids to hang out and have fun.

G ✺

GENERAL ASSEMBLY is the top legislative body of the Presbyterian Church USA. Consisting of both lay and clergy delegates from around the country, the General Assembly meets to discuss and vote on decisions of import to the national church. The comparable legislative body for Episcopalians is General Convention, for United Church of Christ and Methodists is General Conference, for Lutheran is Churchwide Assembly, and for American Baptists is the Biennial Meeting.

GENERAL CONFERENCE. See General Assembly.

GENERAL CONVENTION. See General Assembly.

GOOD NEWS is one of the meanings of the word gospel. In this broader sense, gospel/good news means the message of salvation and the kingdom of God that Christ brought to humankind. What I often hear in this phrase is an expression of the joy in life that many people feel their Christian spiritual practice has brought them.

GOSPEL refers to the Scripture readings taken from the first four books of the New Testament. In its broader sense it means the glad tidings of salvation and the kingdom of God that Christ brought to man.

H–I ✺

HOMILY. See Sermon.

INCLUSIVE is a word churches use when they want to indicate that welcoming different types of people, including but not restricted to gays and lesbians, is central to their identity as a congregation.

J–L ✌

LGBT is shorthand for lesbian, gay, bisexual and transgendered folks.

LAITY OR LAY PEOPLE are the non-ordained members of the church.

LEAD CLERGY is another term for the pastor in charge of an individual congregation.

LITURGICAL describes anything connected with public worship. The liturgical style of a congregation is their habitual way of worshipping together.

LITURGY refers to both an individual public worship ritual as well as to the collection of prescribed forms for religious services of all kinds. So you can talk about the Sunday morning liturgy this week and you can also talk about the liturgy for the whole six-week season of Lent.

M–O ✌

MAINLINE refers to the biggest and longest established Protestant traditions. Mainline denominations trace their histories back to the Protestant Reformation, have individual congregations throughout the country, and have national governing structures.

MINISTER is most often used to mean a person who is authorized to conduct religious worship. In this sense, the word is used interchangeably with pastor and clergy and generally means someone who has been ordained. Many churches also use the word "minister" in reference to lay people who perform certain services in the church community. For example, you could have a youth minister who is not ordained.

NON-CREEDAL refers to a religion in which there is no creed, or statement of religious beliefs that are supposed to be commonly held by all members of that religion. Denominations that are non-creedal, therefore, generally make a point of allowing their members freedom of individual belief.

ORDAIN is to confer holy orders on, or to invest with ministerial or sacramental functions. In every religion, there are certain things that only ordained clergy are empowered to do, especially sacramental functions, such as presiding at a Eucharist, performing marriages, baptizing people.

P–Q

PARISH is another word for individual church. Some denominations don't use this word much and in others there is a technical definition of parish that some individual churches do not match. I use it in the most general sense in this book as interchangeable with congregation.

PASTOR means a minister or priest in charge of a church. It is also used as a title for ordained clergy in certain denominations, e.g., Pastor Smith.

PRESBYTERY is the local level of church authority in the Presbyterian Church. The local presbyteries are the San Jose Presbytery and the San Francisco Presbytery.

PRIEST is an ordained clergy person, most commonly in the Roman Catholic and Episcopal traditions.

R–T

RECONCILING. See Welcoming.

RECTOR is the priest in charge of an Episcopal parish. You might also hear the word "vicar" for an Episcopal priest when the congregation is a mission, which receives financial support from the diocese, rather than an independent parish.

SACRAMENTS are defined in the Episcopal Book of Common Prayer as outward and visible signs of inward and spiritual grace, given by Christ as sure and certain means by which we receive that grace. They are sacred rituals, two of which—Baptism and the Lord's Supper or Holy Communion—are common to all Protestant denominations.

SAME-SEX BLESSING is a liturgy or ritual in which an ordained clergy person blesses the relationship between two individuals of the same gender. Most national churches have not officially approved same-sex blessings, which are also referred to as same-sex unions. (They aren't exactly the same, perhaps, but many people use the terms interchangeably.)

SANCTUARY means, among other things, the main worship space in a church.

SEMINARIAN is someone who is studying in a theological school to become ordained as a clergy person.

SERMON is another word for homily, the talk the pastor or minister gives to the congregation as part of a worship service. Sermons often relate to the Scripture readings from the service and are generally designed to give people food for thought and to help them integrate the message of the readings into their daily lives as Christians in the world.

SERVICE BOOKLET is a printed publication that is your guide to a worship service. Sometimes it tells you where else to go—to the prayer book or hymnal, for instance—to find what you need to participate. At other times the service booklet you are given will have everything you need contained in it.

SYNOD is the local level of church authority in Lutheran Churches. The ECLA congregations in the Bay Area belong to the Sierra Pacific Synod, which includes both northern California and Nevada.

U–Z 🕮

WELCOMING is used by congregations and other groups who want to make a public and clearly understood statement that they fully accept LGBT folks. It is used in combination or interchangeably with affirming, inclusive, and reconciling. There are some nuanced distinctions between these four words, which are discussed in more depth in Chapter Five.

WORSHIP is what people do when they get together as a Christian community on Sunday mornings. It involves prayer, reflection on Bible readings, sometimes celebration of Holy Communion, most often singing. The purpose is to pay reverence to God and to give strength to each other. Worship can be used as either a verb or a noun, when it is most commonly paired with service.

CHURCH INDEX

A

Advent Lutheran Church, Morgan Hill, 163

Albany United Methodist Church, Albany, 108, 119, 122, 132, 138, 144, 176

Aldersgate United Methodist Church, Palo Alto, 167

Aldersgate United Methodist Church, San Rafael, 184

Aldersgate United Methodist Church, South San Francisco, 153

All Saints Lutheran Church, Cupertino, 163

All Saints Lutheran Church, Novato, 183

All Saints' Episcopal Church, Palo Alto, 109, 114, 119, 122, 124, 127, 132, 138, 141, 144, 161

All Saints' Episcopal Church, San Francisco, 104, 106, 107, 108, 112, 121, 122, 124, 127, 130, 138, 141, 144, 156

All Saints' Episcopal Church, San Leandro, 171

All Souls Parish, Berkeley, 171

Allen Temple Baptist Church, Oakland, 179

Almaden Hills United Methodist Church, San Jose, 167

Almaden Valley United Church of Christ, San Jose, 109, 112, 116, 127, 130, 132, 169

Alum Rock United Methodist Church, San Jose, 119, 122, 124, 127, 132, 141, 144, 167

Antioch Baptist Church, San Jose, 170

Arlington Community United Church of Christ, Kensington, 177

Asbury United Methodist Church, Livermore, 104, 109, 112, 114, 116, 127, 134, 135, 137, 138, 176

B

Berkeley Fellowship of Unitarian Universalists, Berkeley, 189

Berkeley Friends Church, Berkeley, 190

Berkeley Monthly Meeting, Berkeley, 191

Beth Eden Baptist Church, Oakland, 108, 109, 112, 116, 130, 137, 138, 179

Bethany Presbyterian Church, San Bruno, 152

Bethany United Methodist Church, San Francisco, 104, 108, 112, 115, 119, 122, 127, 132, 134, 135, 138, 141, 144, 159

Bethel Baptist Church, Novato, 185

Bethel Community Presbyterian Church, San Leandro, 109, 115, 116, 128, 130, 132, 134, 138, 140, 174

Bethel Lutheran Church, Cupertino, 163

Bethlehem Lutheran Church, Oakland, 172

Broadmoor Community United Church of Christ, San Leandro, 177

Broadmoor Presbyterian Church, Daly City, 116, 124, 130, 132, 138, 140, 141, 153

Buena Vista United Methodist Church, Alameda, 176

Burlingame United Methodist Church, Burlingame, 153

C

Calvary Lutheran Church, Millbrae, 152

Calvary Presbyterian Church, Berkeley, 174

College Heights United Church of
Christ, San Mateo, 120, 122, 125,
128, 130, 134, 136, 137, 138, 140,
142, 144, 146, 154

Community Baptist Church, San
Francisco, 160

Community Baptist Church, San
Mateo, 155

Community Church, Hayward, 179

Community Church of Mill Valley,
104, 109, 125, 128, 130, 132, 142,
146, 184

Community Congregational Church of
Belvedere-Tiburon, 185

Community Presbyterian Church, San
Geronimo, 183

Community Presbyterian Church,
Stinson Beach, 183

Community United Church of Christ,
Oakland, 177

Community United Church of Christ,
San Carlos, 154

Congregational Church of Belmont ,
105, 106, 109, 115, 120, 122, 125,
128, 130, 132, 134, 137, 138, 140,
141, 142, 144, 146, 154

Congregational Church of Campbell,
169

Congregational Church of San Mateo,
108, 109, 112, 114, 117, 122, 125,
128, 142, 144, 146, 154

Cosmopolitan Baptist Church,
Oakland, 179

Cosmopolitan Baptist Church, San
Francisco, 160

Cosmopolitan Evangelical United
Church of Christ, San Jose, 169

Court Street United Methodist
Church, Alameda, 176

Covenant Presbyterian Church, Palo
Alto, 105, 112, 115, 117, 138, 146,
165

Covenant Presbyterian Church, San
Francisco, 105, 117, 122, 125, 135,
138, 142, 144, 158

Crosswalk Community Church,
Sunnyvale, 170

Crystal Springs United Methodist
Church, San Mateo, 153

D

Daly City United Methodist Church,
153

Double Rock Baptist Church, San
Francisco, 160

Downs Memorial United Methodist
Church, Oakland, 176

E

Ebenezer Lutheran Church ,San
Francisco, 157

Eden United Church of Christ,
Hayward, 112, 117, 120, 122, 128,
140, 144, 178

El Cerrito United Methodist Church,
181

El Sobrante United Methodist Church,
181

Elmhurst Presbyterian Church,
Oakland, 174

Elmhurst United Methodist Church,
Oakland, 176

Episcopal Church in the Almaden, San
Jose, 162

Episcopal Church of Our Saviour,
Oakland, 171

Episcopal Church of St. Mary the
Virgin, San Francisco, 105, 106,
108, 109, 112, 114, 117, 122, 134,
138, 144, 156

Episcopal Church of the Epiphany, San
Carlos, 151

Starr King Unitarian Universalist Church, Hayward, 189

Stone Church of Willow Glen, San Jose, 166

Strawberry Creek Monthly Meeting, Berkeley, 191

Sunnyhills United Methodist Church, Milpitas, 116, 121, 124, 130, 134, 146, 168

Sunset Ministry, Baptist, San Francisco, 119, 136, 140, 161

T

Taylor Memorial United Methodist Church, Oakland, 177

Temple Baptist Church, San Francisco, 161

Temple Baptist Church, Richmond, 181

Third Baptist Church, San Francisco, 161

Thornton Avenue Baptist Church, Fremont, 180

Thousand Oaks Baptist Church, Berkeley, 180

Transfiguration Episcopal Church, San Mateo, 152

Trinity Baptist Church, San Mateo, 155

Trinity Episcopal Church, San Francisco, 107, 108, 121, 124, 127, 144, 146, 157

Trinity Episcopal Parish, Menlo Park, 152

Trinity Lutheran Church, Alameda, 106, 111, 114, 116, 119, 121, 124, 132, 134, 136, 140, 146, 173

Trinity Lutheran Church, Oakland, 107, 116, 121, 124, 127, 132, 134, 135, 136, 140, 144, 146, 173

Trinity Presbyterian Church, San Carlos, 153

Trinity Presbyterian Church, San Jose, 106, 107, 109, 111, 116, 119, 167

Trinity United Methodist Church, Berkeley, 109, 116, 121, 124, 127, 130, 134, 136, 140, 144, 146, 169, 177

Twenty-First Avenue Baptist Church, Baptist, San Francisco, 141, 161

Twin Towers United Methodist Church, Alameda, 177

U

Union Presbyterian Church, Los Altos, 167

Unitarian Fellowship of Los Gatos, 189

Unitarian Universalist Church of Berkeley, 189

Unitarian Universalist Congregation of Marin, San Rafael, 190

Unitarian Universalist Fellowship, Redwood City, 189

Unitarian Universalist Fellowship of Sunnyvale, 190

Unitarian Universalists of San Mateo, 190

United Church of Christ, Tiburon, 109, 112, 117, 120, 122, 125, 128, 130, 132, 134, 136, 138, 142, 144, 185

United Church of Hayward United Church of Christ, 179

United Lutheran Church of Oakland, 174

United Methodist Church, Berkeley, 177

United Methodist Church of Daly City, 119, 121, 124, 132, 137, 146, 153

University Lutheran Chapel, Berkeley, 109, 111, 119, 121, 124, 127, 132, 135, 140, 144, 146, 174

BARBARA STEVENSON is a baby boomer who grew up in an observant Irish Catholic household. After thirteen years of parochial school (even kindergarten!) she stopped going to church altogether as soon as she moved out of her parents' house to live away at college. In 1991, when her daughter was two years old, Stevenson began to look for a church she thought she could stomach for the sake of her child. She found St. Aidan's Episcopal Church, where you can wear shorts to the Sunday service if you want and no one inquires very closely into anyone's literal beliefs. She has been going to church practically every Sunday ever since. She lives with her husband and two children in San Francisco.